The Technique

The Technique of Persuasion

SIR DAVID NAPLEY

Solicitor of the Supreme Court;
Past President of the Law Society; Director
and Past President of the British Academy of Forensic Sciences

With a Foreword by
The Hon. Mr. Justice Melford Stevenson

FOURTH EDITION

London: Sweet & Maxwell: 1991

First Edition 1970
Second Impression 1971
Second Edition 1975
Second Impression 1977
Third Impression 1980
Third Edition 1983
Fourth Edition 1991
Second Impression 2003

Published by Sweet & Maxwell Limited of
South Quay Plaza, 183 Marsh Wall, London E14 9FT
Phototypeset by LBJ Enterprises Limited, of Chilcompton and Tadley
Printed by TJ International Ltd, Padstow, Cornwall

A catalogue record
for this book is available
from the British Library

ISBN 0–421–43340–X

To

SIR THOMAS LUND, C.B.E.

for his outstanding contribution
to Law and Lawyers

Foreword

I have read this book with real regret. In the late nineteen-twenties, when I first tried to earn a living at the Bar, there was no book of the quality and practical value of Mr. David Napley's work. Such books on advocacy as existed often provoked—and deserved—hollow laughter.

How grateful I and my contemporaries would have been for *The Technique of Persuasion.*

It is true we had the advantage denied to our successors today, of waiting some years before serious work came our way and during those years we learned our job—or did not. We were not nourished on the cornucopia of legal aid.

In the London area, at least, the judiciary at all levels did not always exhibit the benevolent patience so characteristic of contemporary judicial figures. The lessons which can be painlessly learned by anyone who reads Mr. Napley's pages with attention were all too often rubbed in by sharp and ferocious rebukes administered in public by men who were overworked, underpaid and sometimes embittered by the belief that their undoubted ability had not received the reward they hoped for in their chosen profession. (See Mr. Napley's passage on the elements of psychology and their significance).

The discomfort of many of bus journey back to the Temple from a county or magistrates' court was often increased by a painful appraisal of the kind of mistake which is analysed and explained in this book. In this way we learned to present at least the appearance of that humility of which Mr. Napley rightly emphasises the importance.

Humility is a quality not always inborn in those who dedicate themselves to advocacy.

Not the least valuable part of this valuable book is that devoted to the preparation of cases. I shall always be glad that before going to the Bar I spent a year in the litigation department of a firm of solicitors where I became familiar with at least some of the matters which do not ordinarily come to the notice of the beginner at the Bar, and I am indeed grateful to the experienced managing clerks who introduced them to me. Managing clerks of the kind I used to know seem to be an almost extinct race but all and more than I managed to learn is set out in this book.

I hope no one will be discouraged by the fact that Mr. Napley's work is full of counsels of perfection. Those who use it will find that their early performances will fall well below the author's standard.

I recommend a re-reading of the book at regular intervals.

May I end by saying that few qualities in an advocate appeal so powerfully to a judge as brevity.

I fear this foreword has already transgressed in this respect.

MELFORD STEVENSON

Preface to Fourth Edition

When this small book first appeared over twenty years ago, I was gratified to note that it received uniformly favourable reviews—with one exception. A Scottish Silk greeted it with scorn, remarking, in terms, that it was ridiculous to write a book explaining the advantage, when noting evidence at a trial, in underlining points for cross-examination with one colour pencil and points for final argument with a different colour pencil. This book, however, was created as, and remains primarily, an introduction to advocacy for those who have little or no experience of it; too often matters which may seem trivial in the extreme are overlooked by the tyro, and even the more mature, only because they do appear trivial. What has happened since, is that the book has now reached its fourth edition and meanwhile I have forgotten the name of the Scottish Silk.

Amongst such suggestions as have been offered to me has been that I might deal with the procedural changes which have occurred since the last edition and, in particular, such matters as the Police and Criminal Evidence Act. This however, is not a book about procedure and once embarked upon that course, the whole nature and character of the work would change.

The need to inform oneself about basic principles of advocacy has, with the proposed changes in the rights of audience, become far more important for solicitors than was formerly the case. I have revised the text with that in mind, but, for the most part, sound advocacy differs little in its essentials, whether conducted in the magistrates', county or High Courts. Persuasion necessarily involves creating the requisite interest in, and the acceptance of, your arguments in the minds of those you seek to persuade; success as an advocate does not primarily depend upon the status of the audience, but the skill and quality of the persuader.

DAVID NAPLEY

Preface to Fourth Edition

Preface to First Edition

This small book is not presented as an elixir of advocacy which, taken in suitable doses, will turn the halting phrases of the inexperienced advocate to pure gold. It represents no more than revised versions of talks given by the author to the Associate and Young Members of the Law Society. However, sufficient appreciation was expressed concerning them to galvanise a few members of the audience into initiating courses of training in advocacy which have now become an established part of the facilities offered by the Law Society under the control of its Education and Training Committee.

A number of persons, including Mr. Justice Melford Stevenson, who has been kind enough to add a Foreword to this book, urged that the talks should be published in book form, This small work therefore appears in response to that request.

To the experienced advocate, much of it may well appear to be trite and platitudinous. One has learned, however, that what, with experience and in retrospect, appears so obvious, is far from apparent to the tyro.

Apart from the author's own experience in the courts, he has had the advantage, over many years, of sitting behind others while they have pursued the art of advocacy. It has been a rewarding experience; ranging between enthralment whilst the technique was displayed by acknowledged masters such as the late Sir Norman Birkett, Sir Patrick Hastings, Sergeant Sullivan and many other great advocates, to purgatory while some less great advocate expressed to the court what he believed to be the law—the author then joning, not too ostentatiously, in the general merriment which followed. Thus, what is here written may also be of assistance to young barristers. Unhappily, there are some courts in which police officers are still required to act as advocates, and it may well be of some assistance to them.

In short, it is a distillation, within a very small container, of over thirty-five years observation and practice of the technique of persuasion. If, as a result, it provides a measure of guidance and confidence to the beginner and enables him to avoid some of the errors into which the author fell at the outset of his professional life, its publication will have been justified. If it should encourage those who have not ventured into this field to experience the excitement and satisfaction—to say nothing of the occasional despair—which the practice of this technique involves, it will have been doubly worth the effort of recording it.

London
November 1969 DAVID NAPLEY

Contents

I: Preparation for Trial

Introduction

It happens from design, and not by chance, that the title is "The technique of persuasion" and not, as have been so many before it, "The art of advocacy," or even, in keeping with the modern trend, "The anatomy of advocacy." When one speaks of advocacy, the mind turns to presenting a case in court—admittedly a form at once the most skilled and dramatic. That, however, is only part of my subject. As Lord Macmillan reminded us in *Law and Other Things*, and as many before and since have remarked, the practice of advocacy is a pursuit by which those who follow it seek to persuade.

I have rejected the title "The art of advocacy" for other reasons. In the first place because the use of the terms "art" (although not so defined in the Oxford Dictionary) conjures to one's mind a natural gift rather than an acquired skill; it gives support to those—whose views I do not share—that many of the essentials of advocacy cannot be taught. Admittedly the truly great advocates—the Marshall Halls, the Norman Birketts and other forensic giants—were especially gifted from birth but the vast preponderance of skilled and successful advocates have done little more than acquire a technique; and one, at that, which any person of reasonable intelligence and aptitude can acquire by patience, application and practice.

My second reason for rejecting that title is to disabuse, from the outset, the belief that advocacy for the lawyer is something to be practised only in a court of law, on one's feet, cross-examining witnesses or persuading a judge, if not to decide in one's favour, then at least to keep awake and listen. As a moment's reflection will remind you, virtually all tasks undertaken by lawyers on behalf of clients are for the most part, themselves a form of advocacy—the employment of the technique of persuasion. The common lawyer who seeks to negotiate a settlement is an advocate of his client's interests and cause; the conveyancer who negotiates a contract or lease is an advocate, seeking to persuade others to the acceptance of terms more favourable to his client; the company lawyer who guides or conducts his client's affairs at a company or any other meeting must call in aid the technique of persuasion; even the writing of solicitors' letters, other than those of a purely formal nature, involves, to a greater or less degree, some use of advocacy. Indeed, were I required to single out one attribute which the practising lawyer must possess to lift him from the average to the class of the more skilled and efficient, I would unhesitatingly choose the skill to be found in applying the technique of persuasion, or, in other words, advocacy.

It is, in these circumstances, the more surprising that the curriculum designed for those who seek to practise as lawyers previously contained no instruction—or indeed guidance—in this most fundamental of all legal skills.*

It follows that I have no intention of occupying time with the bones which make up the anatomy of so many articles and books, each delightfully, amusingly and unremuneratively written, on advocacy. I have no intention of enjoining you to stand up, speak up and sit down—although you should do all three. Nor shall I implore you to play up and play the game, for I am sure you will; nor even cajole you to emulate the great advocates of the past, the like of which in any event, in changed conditions, are unlikely to be seen again. Rather, in a limited space shall I hope to examine with you the essential know-how of our profession—the most effective way to persuade.

In the 21 years which have passed since the first edition of this book appeared, great changes have been promised, even if they are never completely fulfilled, in the structure of the profession of the law, particularly as it affects advocacy. Before too long, solicitors—albeit an insufficient number—will appear as advocates in the higher courts. Even those with considerable experience of advocacy in the lower courts, will share, with barristers newly called to the Bar, the sense of apprehension at the prospect of conducting cases before High Court judges.

Some may regard it as presumptious for one who has, out of necessity, only had experience of addressing the

* The Bar has since amended its curriculum to include Advocacy, and the Education and Training Committee of the Council of the Law Society has taken over the conduct of, and responsibility for, the advocacy courses of which that talk was the forerunner.

higher judiciary when they were sitting in chambers, offering advice as to advocacy before the High Court. However, whilst the only way in which to acquire the requisite skill is by actually undertaking it, yet, over the fifty seven or so years since the Author entered the profession as an articled clerk, the process of observing and selecting others to perform that task, has, at least, provided the justification for offering guidance.

Advocacy is advocacy, and good or bad advocacy is exactly that, at which ever level it is performed. The underlying principles do not change with the status of the Tribunal. As will later emerge, in the planning of one's treatment of, and tactics for, the presentation of the particular case, one must have regard to the requirements practice, and manner of proceeding in whichever forum you may find yourself.

It might be thought that the higher the court and the greater the skill of the Judges, the faster, as a consequence, it will proceed. Paradoxically, it is precisely the contrary. In the magistrates courts, the pressure of work is such that the Bench is more responsive to the advocate who appears to advance his case with the greatest speed, whilst avoiding, in the process, omitting those aspects which it is vital to cover. The County Court, whilst still abhorring the wasting of time, proceeds rather more slowly and the High Court has always tended to proceed at even a slower pace than the courts below it.

Clearly, there is a world of difference between the way a Bench of lay magistrates should be addressed from the way in which one would deal with a trained lawyer. There is, however, no more to be feared when presenting a case to a High Court judge than when appearing before any other lawyer. All of them will regard your presence with greater warmth, if they feel your prowess is such that you are able to assist them in their own endeavours to avoid making mistakes.

If I were given a free hand in settling a new syllabus for the examinations of lawyers, I would first render it compulsory for every candidate to have studied, and undertaken an examination in, the elements of psychology—the science of human behaviour. For generations psychology has been, and to some extent still remains, for some lawyers, a dirty word—the vapouring of so many cranks. Yet, in truth, some knowledge of it lies at the very root of all successful endeavour, essential in effective cross-examination; it is an integral part of skilled negotiation; it is indispensable in the field of public relations; in short, it is the lifeblood of successful practice as a lawyer. It is also, incidentally, the one subject which every article on advocacy, however, discursive, and every book, however erudite, studiously avoids.

When I qualified as a solicitor (and it may be as well to mention that I did so, if only to remove any emerging doubt), I was able, through the persistence and art of my teachers, to recite the rules both in *Shelley's Case* and *Allhusen* v. *Whittell*. Fortunately no-one then or since has asked me to explain what they decided. No-one, on the other hand, ever pointed out the wisdom, before addressing lay magistrates, of ascertaining the nature of their occupations. I had myself to discover from experience, the persuasive force of drawing similes from the everyday activities of the particular magistrates or of others whom one was anxious to influence.

Psychology involves, in common parlance, finding out "what makes people tick." All of us share, in differing degrees, certain basic needs, wants and desires. A need to survive and dominate; a desire to be loved or admired; a wish to be feared or respected; a wish to be knowledgeable—and to be thought knowledgeable in particular skills and pursuits. We are, in some ways aggressive, and in others, submissive, and this obtains both sexually and in other ways.

To seek to persuade without understanding how these traits and virtues manifest themselves is comparable to driving a car without discovering how it works. It is wholly legitimate, in the pursuit of advocacy, to turn to its fullest account a knowledge of the psychology of those you seek to persuade. That—indeed—is much of what the technique of persuasion is about. This is hardly the place, however, in which to embark upon a study of psychology or to do more than underline its cardinal importance in dictating your choice of action as a lawyer.

How many lawyers, for example, pause to consider the simple fact that dislike of an individual will often extend to dislike of his opinions? Yet there are still those who believe it clever to behave in an aggressive and even offensive fashion towards the opposing party and even his legal representatives. Some even adopt the same attitude with the court which they are addressing. This involves more than a lack of courtesy, which any of us can readily recognise; it reflects an absence of appreciation of the first essentials of simple psychology.

Man, the psychologists tell us, includes among his basic wants and needs the desire to be appreciated and applauded by his fellows; he is gratified by the recognition of his own skill and ability and, whatever you may have been told to the contrary, judges are still human. Thus most experienced advocates are mindful of the advantage to be gained by insinuating into the mind of a judge some point which assists their case, under conditions where he satisfies his own ego in the belief that the point was one which he had alone discovered, which is decisive, and which everyone else had overlooked.

When the judge has failed to grasp the argument which an advocate has expounded with clarity and precision it is inappropriate to point out—more particularly in a crowded court—that the judge is muddled and has failed to grasp the essentials of a simple proposition. This certainly will not accord with his desire to be admired and appreciated, and is more calculated to bring into action the underlying aggression in his nature. How much wiser to agree that he must be correct, but to suggest that it might be expressed somewhat differently, and then repeat the proposition, suitably corrected. Moreover never underestimate the likely psychological responses, or the level of discernment, of those you are seeking to persuade. The advocate who is constantly outstripping his opponent with clever legal points or objections is likely to enlist only sympathy for his adversary, whilst an evident desire to assist his opponent, and the court, tends to indicate how strong he considers his own case to be. So as different facets of advocacy are examined, the value of a regard for the underlying psychology will become increasingly apparent.

Closely linked to an understanding of the psychology of the judge you are addressing, and of your own, is the imperative need for self confidence. Experienced advocates soon come to understand this. In his introduction to the first edition of this book, the late Sir Melford Stevenson, who was himself an accomplished and highly experienced advocate and later an equally highly experienced High Court Judge commented "Humility is a quality not always inborn in those who dedicate themselves to advocacy." This is undoubtedly true, but may well derive from constant endeavour to present what they have to say as being unquestionably and indisputably correct. Confidence is essential, but when it evolves into arrogance and conceit to the exclusion of humility it is time for the advocate to take a long rest and reexamines his values.

Confidence is to be achieved by a knowledge that you have complete mastery of the facts, law and tactics of your case, and this, in its turn, brings an additional advantage. Given that you have achieved, in relation to the task in hand that level of justified confidence, you also then realise that you have a considerable lead over the judge himself. He will, at the outset, know nothing about the case, whilst you are familiar, or so you hope, with every aspect of it. This should do much towards alleviating your sense of apprehension.

In measuring the likely judicial approach, as you must, you will apply your knowledge of psychology in a meaningful, yet basic, way to the judge himself. Never allow yourself to feel intimidated by his undoubted knowledge, ability or status, although you will always extend courtesy whilst deferring to the important office which he holds. In reality he responds to virtually the same impulses, pressures and conditions as most of the other human beings you have met. Experience demonstrates this. Thus, however strong your case in law, and even in essential facts, if your client, the plaintiff, is shown to be unworthy, dishonest or, himself, lacking in merit, it will be no surprise if the judge, mentally, finds himself anxious to find against him. Certainly, it has been said of one eminent judge that even after he had formulated his judgment, his judicial colleagues soon learned that his views could be changed if he was assured that the person in whose favour he would otherwise have decided was a frightful cad. Never be too dewy eyed about the utter impartiality of Justice; judges can be fallible like the rest of us.

In the criminal courts, the judiciary undoubtably make a special effort to steel themselves against allowing their personal feelings and reactions to colour their judgment. Whether all of them always succeed may be in question. As an advocate you are always entitled by fair, proper and admissible means to make whatever you properly can of the unworthiness of the opposing party, unless of course you are prosecuting in a criminal matter, where such evidence is generally inadmissible.

Again, from the psychological aspect, you should take into account, and distinguish, attitudes and opinions. The former are usually long lived, and frequently reflect the background, family, or group in which an individual is nurtured. If you have knowledge of such influences you have a powerful adjuct to the process of persuasion, and can adjust the thrust, manner and tone of your argument to meet and compensate for it. Opinion, on the other hand, may be more briefly held, and thus may be more amenable to change. It is always wise to try to learn in advance the opinions currently held by those you seek to persuade, and again, adjust your presentation to cater for them.

One psychological factor which can be valuable in this regard is that of suggestibility. It is often better to suggest a desirable possibility then to present it with stark directness. The mind often reacts more to the processes of its own reasoning faculties then to those produced from the mind of another.

Important in the field of suggestability is the standing or seniority of the person seeking to persuade. Suggestions from such sources frequently find easier acceptability. This is, perhaps, the major justification for the engagement of Leading Counsel; their suggestions tend, human nature being what it is, to carry greater weight than those of less exalted advocates. Not least of the areas in which the instilling of ideas by suggestion has particular value, as will be later seen, arises when presenting mitigation.

An important lesson, therefore, to be learned in the immediate future is that what will be required, under the forthcoming scheme of things in the High Court, is not one whit different from what an advocate should expect to display in any other court, namely a carefully prepared, tactically sound and clear case, upon which an adequate amount of care and thought has been expended. In this, an understanding of the first principles of simple psychology will materially assist.

The objectives

Let us then endeavour to break down the essentials of persuasion.

The first and vital aspect is clearly the objective. Of course, every lawyer who undertakes a case for a client knows the object is to win; that is certainly the client's objective. Yet I am sure we would be amazed, if such matters could be investigated, how many lawyers pursue their daily tasks without ever asking themselves the simple questions, "Must I destroy the whole fabric of my opponent's case, or only parts of it, and, if so which?" "What am I seeking to achieve by this exercise?"

The next stage is to determine and preferably to note on paper what you have to prove or disprove. If your client's claim lies in negligence, you must establish that the defendant owed a duty of care, that he failed to exercise that degree of care expected of a reasonable man, and that, as a result, your client has suffered damage. The time to decide how you are going to prove or disprove these matters is at the outset—not halfway through or just before the trial itself. This may sound platitudinous, but too many solicitors begin to prepare for trial (as, incidentally, the costs precedents seem to suggest) only when they come to prepare the brief to counsel or their own minutes of fact and argument; too many wait to obtain, at a relatively late stage, an opinion on evidence from counsel. If this is to be done, that is far too late to do it. In any event, a competent solicitor should not need counsel or anyone else to tell him what is necessary to prove his client's case. The collation of the relevant evidence and knowledge of what should and may be proved is especially his task. Indeed, it is at this stage of initial analysis that you can demonstrate the difference between the pedestrian practitioner and the specially skilled. The latter never accepts anything on its face value. Do not, therefore, accept that because a text book asserts the law to be one thing it cannot, in fact, be another. Examine the problem from a different angle.

Thus, as it is hoped will later be seen, it is from an appreciation of the law applicable, the understanding of what must be proved or can be disproved or nullified, and the exclusion of all aspects which can safely be omitted with a view to the maximum simplification that you can determine your tactics in the case.

Preparation of the case

Only when you have clearly defined your objective, and what you must establish to achieve it, can you turn to the serious business of preparation which, I venture to suggest but which books on advocacy hitherto have rarely stressed, constitutes the overwhelmingly important part of the art of advocacy and the technique of persuasion.

Research into the Law

It too often has been suggested especially of late that the Bar, as specialists, are necessarily better advocates and lawyers than solicitors. The impression is given that they are lone wolves working single-handed to achieve success for their clients. In fact, the young barrister, when he goes to the Bar, is in no better position than the young solicitor to know whether or not advocacy is his metier. Moreover, today both solicitors and barristers are drawn from the same intellectual and educational pool.

The average barrister, however—unlike, I regret to say, some solicitors—learns never to give an opinion without first looking up his law. By comparison the solicitor, who currently works under greater pressures over a wider field, often labours under the false impression that if his client—being a layman—sees him looking at books before answering his questions, he will assume that he does not know his job and will lose confidence. Yet, if a solicitor wishes to attain real proficiency in his profession, he must take time to check his law. It should be the solicitor's objective to use counsel, as far as possible, only in those cases where points of law require prolonged research, which the nature of the case or of his practice renders it impossible to undertake, or where a second opinion is required. Where counsel is employed this should never deter the solicitor from conducting his own preliminary research; he should propound the legal questions which require elucidation and set down, for consideration and discussion, the arguments which might be best advanced in furtherance of the client's cause. This recommendation is not in any way directed to reducing the volume of work going to the Bar. No student of the law can hope to carry his detailed knowledge of the text books through his professional life without constantly replenishing and widening his stock of knowledge.

The barrister must constantly refer to and quote the authorities. If the solicitor leaves this task exclusively to the barrister his legal knowledge—and thus his value as an advocate—must diminish with each passing year.

So, wherever the opportunity arises, the solicitor as well as the barrister should do his own research and form his own opinions—as he must inevitably do if he intends to practise advocacy in the courts.

In one respect the task of the solicitor as an advocate in defending criminal cases in the lower courts is more difficult than that of the barrister who conducts his advocacy under conditions where he is fully informed in the higher courts of the prosecution evidence; by contrast, much of the solicitor's advocacy in criminal cases must be performed in the dark. Under the present procedure he is not apprised of the case he needs to meet until the evidence is called before the court; this impairs the quality of the advocacy and perhaps as a result, of justice and needs to be rectified.

Importance of Preparation

A carefully prepared case may be brought to a successful conclusion by one who, by nature or otherwise, is a poor advocate when on his feet; but an inadequately prepared case is unlikely to be won unless presented by an unusually able advocate, one one of his lucky days, before either a singularly good or a singularly bad judge. There has never been a great advocate who could have achieved his position without the conscientious preparation which must have gone into the case before it was presented to the court, and what I desire to stress is that the solicitor should normally decide at a fairly early stage in the case the use to which the relevant information is to be put.

The presentation of a client's case, whether to a court of law, to a company meeting or elsewhere, necessarily involves two distinct parts: the preparation and the presentation itself. It is, of course, impossible to express with precision the relative importance of these two aspects of advocacy and persuasion. Yet it can be said with little fear of contradiction that while both parts are vital, the extent and quality of preparation is infinitely more important, significant and essential than the manner of presentation. Both, of course, benefit from the acquisition of special skills and experience. Sometimes laymen, lacking both, succeed in cases from the county court to the House of Lords, against the cream of advocates, simply because they devote themselves to thorough preparation, by which they seek out and present the decisive and essential evidence. It can rarely if ever occur, however, that the most skilled advocate can succeed where the work of preparation has been shoddy, incompetent or inadequate.

Reading the biographies of great advocates of the past, you are left with the clear impression that the ultimate success rested wholly upon their consummate skill and eloquence. Impressive witnesses were broken in the witness box by no more than a series of brilliantly contrived questions; lost causes were won by no more than the charm of the silver tongued counsel. Every hour of the day stupendous feats were performed which, on television, even Perry Mason could attain only once a week. What part, then, had been played by preparation?

Secure for yourself those books—in the Notable British Trials series or elsewhere—in which you can read outstanding cross-examinations. Many are to be found in biographies which understandably extol the trial abilities of outstanding advocates. Ask yourself, as you read, how much of this cross-examination could have proceeded had the cross-examiner been denied the material with which to confound the witness. Yet biographies and books on advocacy rarely, if ever, explain how the preparatory side of advocacy should be developed, or its super-abundant importance in that pursuit. Take, for example, the cross-examination in *Tichborne* v. *Lushington*, a case which lasted 101 days in the Common Pleas in 1871. The case, as you well know, was brought to establish that the plaintiff was Roger Tichborne, heir to a baronetcy and the estates of the Tichborne family. While not wishing to deny the undoubted skill displayed by Lord Coleridge, it is quite clear that almost every question designed to discredit the claimant's assertion that he had been educated at Stonyhurst College was based upon long, arduous and painstaking research by the instructing solicitors into the daily happenings at the College, its topography and routine, the school periods of Roger Tichborne, and a thousand and one other details without which hardly a single effective question could have been put in cross-examination.

Similarly, in the trial of Adelaide Bartlett, Mr. Edward Clarke, Q.C., cross-examined a doctor on his findings that the cause of death of the accused's husband was chloroform poisoning, which the prosecution alleged she had administered to him. The forensic medical details, which formed the basis of his questions, and without which they could not have been framed, could only have resulted from research and inquiry, by those preparing the case, with the assistance of competent experienced forensic experts.

A more recent example is to be found in the trial of Mrs. Harvey at Ruthen Assizes in 1960 in a case which has become known as the Rhyl Mummy case. The mummified body of Mrs. Knight, who had been a lodger in Mrs. Harvey's home, was found with a stocking round her neck, which the prosecution alleged had been used as a ligature to murder her. This conclusion was reached by the prosecution's forensic experts because it was embedded into the neck causing a groove of as much as two centimetres, a localised depression on the front of the neck and the flattening of the left lamina of the thyroid cartilage.

The late Professor Camps, who was consulted by the defence, told me that Mrs. Harvey's solicitor and counsel, being convinced of her innocence in regard to the charge of murder, were tireless in their endeavours to investigate and explain the apparently damning forensic evidence. As a result, it was established that Mrs. Knight had been in a late stage of disseminated sclerosis, and that an old custom existed—not limited to the north of England—of tying a stocking (preferably unwashed after use) round the neck, when ill, as a means of achieving recovery from a sore throat or cold.

The question therefore, was whether the stocking had been tightly applied to the neck as a ligature and murder weapon, as the prosecution alleged, or loosely applied by the woman herself before her death. (The accused had said that she found the woman dead and put her body in a cupboard in order to be able to collect her old age pension.) Further scientific evidence was then adduced, based on considerable original research, as to the tensile strength, the distribution of the knitting loops and stitches, and similar matters which favoured the theory that the stocking had been loosely applied before death, and that after death the body gases, etc., had caused the neck to swell, thus producing the groove in the neck. As a result on the fifth day of the trial, the prosecution withdrew the allegation of murder.

May I be permitted—as a final example—to draw upon a case with which I was personally concerned, which resulted in the Home Secretary ordering the Mars-Jones Inquiry.

In August 1959 it was alleged against three young men that they had been found by police officers in London in unlawful possession of offensive weapons, namely two barbers' razors and a weighted rubber hose, suitable for use as a cosh. This they denied, contending from the first moment that they gave me instructions that the weapons had been planted on them by the police. They had no right to demand trial by jury, and the prosecution elected for summary trial; moreover, despite three requests to them to send the case for trial, the magistrates refused to do so.

The three accused asserted that they had been taken to an upstairs part of the police station, and then later, one by one, down to a room for interview—thus facilitating the planting by the police of weapons on them individually. The police officers, who were young aides to C.I.D., insisted that all the defendants had remained together throughout, in the charge room.

Since, under our criminal procedure, the defence in cases tried summarily must (until the recommendations of the Council of the Law Society are implemented, if ever) conduct the hearing without full knowledge of the case they have to meet, we had not, and could not have, anticipated that the police would deny the visit to the upper portion of the police station. Thus, when they did, it became necessary during the course of the hearing to take detailed instructions as to the description of the upper part of the premises and to put this, bit by bit, in cross-examination to the officers. They disputed much of this description, falsely denying, for example, that there was a lavatory on the first floor as the accused alleged.

The lay magistrates, however, convicted the accused and fined them £10 each. They having been advised of the risk of an increased sentence on appeal, decided nevertheless to proceed. I caused the police station to be inspected and discovered that the upstairs conformed in every detail with the description given by the boys, which they could hardly have known had they not been there.

On the hearing of the appeal, the prosecution adduced by way of additional evidence the account of several police officers, including a detective sergeant whose evidence had not been presented in the court below. Those officers purported to corroborate the evidence of the aides to C.I.D. and, on the material then available, it proved impossible effectively to shake their testimony. In the result the convictions of the three youths were upheld, the penalty was increased, and they were each sentenced to one month's imprisonment, which they duly served.

After five years, the Home Secretary was at last persuaded to set up a public inquiry, in the course of which a great deal of documentary and other evidence became available which, under existing procedure, had not been available to the defence either at the original hearing or on the appeal. Thus, the prosecution case had been throughout that the three young men were arrested at 11.15 p.m. outside a public house; that they had been questioned, searched and transported some little distance to a police station at which they arrived at approximately 11.30 p.m. The prosecution had further asserted that the three defendants were in the company of the police sergeant and that he had returned to the police station with them at the same time. Access to police records, however, at the time of the Mars-Jones inquiry, showed that at shortly after 11.15 p.m. the police sergeant had made a call to the country from the police station and that it would have been physically impossible for him and his colleagues to have reached the station with the other officers and the accused at 11.15 p.m., if that was the time the accused had been arrested some distance away. This clearly provided strong corroboration for the story of the accused that they had been arrested at 11.00 p.m. and not 11.15 p.m., and provided additional time for the planting of weapons to have occurred as the accused alleged but the police denied. Access to these records provided many other matters as the subject for fruitful cross-examination, including the hitherto undisclosed fact that in the cars which had taken the accused from the place of arrest to the police station there was another unconnected person suspected of some other offence, who could, at the time, have given valuable evidence as to what occurred en route to the station.

The significance of this example is that although I subjected each of the aides to C.I.D. to a fairly rigorous cross-examination in the magistrates' court, it was quite evident that I failed to convince the magistrates of the unreliability of the police officers. By the same token, counsel who appeared at the appeal was unable to convince that tribunal of the unreliability of the police witnesses, despite his vast experience as a cross-examiner in criminal causes. At the Mars-Jones inquiry, however, when cross-examination was based upon material meanwhile obtained under the new facilities, I, with the other advocates, was able to cross-examine these officers in a far more effective way. By pinning them down to statements previously made, and confronting them with the newly disclosed documents and information, it became possible to show them to be manifestly unreliable witnesses.

This, therefore, demonstrates two important matters. The first, obvious as it may seem, is that the ultimate presentation of a case and its outcome will be significantly assisted by securing the maximum available material in advance of the trial. The more detail which can be unearthed by diligent enquiry concerning the parties, the witnesses, their character and credibility, the background to the dispute, and the scene of the relevant event (which should always be visited where it is clearly relevant, as in motoring cases), the better equipped you will be to conduct the subsequent trial. Unlike America, where the practice is wide-spread, insufficient use is made in this country of in-house enquiry agents in the fields of both civil and criminal litigation.

The second vital truth which emerges is that the real basis for presentation of a case—and the gravamen of the technique of persuasion—is not so much the way in which the case is presented at the hearing in terms of style and experience, whatever the biographers may say (although, of course, no-one would seek to underestimate the importance of these matters). The decisive factor lies in the initial preparation; the material which is so disclosed; the incontrovertible facts which are marshalled; and the care and patience which go into ensuring that no stone is left unturned. These are by far the most significant factors in the proper presentation of the case for any client.

The First Interview

What then, are the essentials of the technique of persuasion? The solicitor, having first ascertained the nature of the client's problem in general terms, should then allow the client to tell his story in his own way, limiting interruptions to a minimum and only using them where some aspect of the matter is not clear. Meanwhile make brief notes, sufficient to keep the main facts in your head, and where he refers to anything which is or may be contained in a document, make sure you get it from him. When he has completed his story, question him closely on any parts of it which strike you as being either unclear, incredible or unlikely, and satisfy yourself as far as possible of the accuracy of what he has told you. This done, take a proof of evidence from the client, assuming, of course, that you believe that he has some sort of case to present. The expression "proof of evidence" means no more than a typed or written account in the first person of the evidence which a witness is able to adduce or impart in relation to the issues arising in the proceedings. One cannot, moreover, too strongly stress the desirability of taking statements from the client and witnesses at the earliest possible opportunity. In the first place, memories tend to fade and events to recede from the minds of the witnesses. In the second place, some vitally important fact may escape your own recollection. In the third place, an important part of the preparation of a case is the protection of the client against himself; frequently a client, when subsequently confronted with an earlier statement which he made to you will deny embarrassing parts of it unless a written record can be produced to him. Some practitioners, with this in mind, insist on the witness reading and correcting the proof himself and then signing it as correct. The first proof taken from a client should, therefore, be in the nature of a draft, not for the purpose of correcting or editing his evidence, but because the proof upon which the trial will ultimately proceed should be in chronological order and free, so far as possible, from ambiguities of language— although again, as far as possible, couched in the terminology of the client himself. Considerable care and skill is involved in the preparation of a good proof of evidence. It is best to record everything the client or witness recounts and not to eliminate material—often highly informative—solely because it will be inadmissible in evidence. Although it must be eliminated at the hearing, it is often of advantage to have readily available the background to some act done or action taken.

16

However, it is wise when finally preparing yourself for the trial to put the inadmissable parts between square brackets, to facilitate the exclusion of such matters from the witness's evidence.

Ensure, moreover, that every proof provides the fullest possible explanation of documentary evidence. Include a simple account of technical aspects which may be meaningful to the witness but wholly unintelligible to the non-technical mind. Where appropriate, explain through the witness the reasons why particular letters were written. Remember to notice whether letters commence by acknowledging or otherwise referring to other letters which have not been produced to you. If that occurs, call for, or otherwise obtain, them.

In short, your objective should be, in producing a proof of evidence, to answer in advance all these questions arising on the proof and accompanying documents which an experienced counsel usually has to put to an inexperienced solicitor when one is instructing him, or which the judge or opposing advocate raises at the hearing, to your astonishment, chagrin and dismay.

Where the narrative is likely to be long and complicated—and particularly in matrimonial proceedings where some degree of embarrassment is often present—it is useful to ask the client to set out the complete history from first to last in his or her own words. When this is received a clear copy is typed and this is used, at a further interview, as the basis for preparing the client's proof in the way already suggested.

When the initial notes or draft proof of evidence has been completed, it will be found useful to note on a piece of paper the essential matters which you will have to prove to establish your client's case, be it by way of prosecution or defence, as plaintiff or defendant. Having decided which legal aspect is involved, look up and note down the facts which you will need to prove—marking with a tick those which are readily capable of such proof, and with a cross those which require further inquiry and research. This is probably best done in tabular form, with the fact to be established in the first column, the evidence available in the second, the witness or source in the third, and action still required, in the last.

Letter before action

It may now become necessary to write what has come to be known as a "letter before action." This is so described in the cost precedents upon which bills of costs are based when a suit has been commenced or concluded. It might, however, be better described as a "letter to avoid action," since that should in truth be its objective—whilst ensuring, if action has to follow, that the letter will further—and not hinder—the client's cause. Thus the writing of such a letter involves to a greater or less degree some use of advocacy. There are those—and there are many of them—who believe, when consulted by a client, that the first essential is to get something into writing and into the hands of the proposed defendant at the earliest possible moment. To them it seems impressive, having heard a hasty account both of the alleged facts and the nature of his complaint from a seething client, to call in a secretary and hurriedly dictate the first letter in what may be an important lawsuit for the client. Impressive it may be: but in the last analysis probably more litigation has been lost by a hasty, ill-considered and ill-prepared letter before action than by any other single factor. Of course it will sometimes happen that a letter must be sent off as a matter of urgency, and insufficient time is available to give it the thought and preparation which, ideally and normally, it requires. But this is likely to be the exception rather than the rule. The proper time at which to send off a letter before action is after you have gone through the procedure I have described: listened to the client's story; checked it; and noted, for your own guidance and clarification, the objectives which you seek to achieve and the essential matters which it will be necessary ultimately to prove in order to secure a decision favourable to your client. In any matter, other than one of trifling importance, it is desirable to prepare a draft of a letter before action. This document will generally represent the first opportunity which your client will have had, with legal advice, to set down the significant facts of his complaint and the basis upon which he proposes to advance it. When we come to examine the presentation of a case to the court itself, it will be seen that the subject-matter of the letter before action can be one of the most fruitful sources of confounding the case for the plaintiff. A skilled cross-examiner can elicit from the plaintiff a series of facts, which he then summarises in as short and concise a manner as is possible. Having done so, he then continues, "And so, Mr. Snoggs, the facts which I have just put to you, and with which you now agree, represent the facts upon which you rely in this case."

"Yes," says Mr. Snoggs, "that is so."

"And, Mr. Snoggs, it is upon the basis of those facts that you are now claiming damages for breach of contract?"

"Yes," replies the unfortunate Mr. Snoggs. The advocate then picks up and hands to the witnesses the agreed bundle of correspondence.

"Mr. Snoggs," he continues, "take these letters in your hand, if you will, and examine the very first letter which was written in this action."

The client looks at the letter, and is required to read it aloud. As he does so, it becomes quite evident that the facts which he has recently recounted on oath to the court are very different from those contained in the letter before action, and that the basis upon which he is advancing his claim has completely changed. He has probably been put into a position from which the average plaintiff finds it difficult to extricate himself, and the court is left with the impression that he has bent the facts in such manner as would best assist his case and that there is really little merit in what he is contending. It is the client who at that stage is discomfited; but the fault is probably that of his lawyer. Had he cleared his own mind as to his client's objectives, and first of all properly investigated and understood the facts—checking their accuracy and relevance—he might never have placed his client in the peril in which he now finds himself, and would not, as will probably then occur, have lost the client's case. In some cases it is probable that he would never have commenced it.

The letter before action, when received by the potential defendant, will probably be taken by him at once to his own solicitor. One of the objects which a skilfully drawn letter before action might achieve is to draw out, in the letter in reply, the probable nature of the defence, so that the counter-arguments and facts may be tested in advance or be refuted in the future. The letter before action needs, therefore, to be phrased with great care.

Thus, in a claim based on a defamatory statement, it may make considerable difference to the extent and nature of future preparation if it can be ascertained whether the answer will be justification, fair comment or a straight denial. The ideal remains, however, that the letter before action should so forcefully but succinctly present the complaint that the recipient decides, or is advised, to proffer a full and unconditional apology.

No less care—and no less regard to the matters applicable to a letter before action—is essential in drafting the letter in reply. Moreover, in the most difficult of cases, a carefully thought out response may go a long way to mitigating the damages or nullifying the claim.

Above all—and constantly—keep in mind the advice which an old lawyer gave—somewhat coldly—to his love-sick son, "Never write any letter without asking yourself as you write it, how will this sound if it is read in court?"

A good precept to apply, in general, is "when in doubt, leave it out."

Proofs of Witnesses

When the real bones of contention have been isolated, proofs should then be taken from any known witnesses and all relevant documents obtained—originals, of course, for preference, since copies are not generally admissible in evidence.

Clients will generally volunteer to scan their files and records, in order to extract for you those which they consider to be relevant to their case. This is an offer which should always be rejected. Too often they are uninformed as to what is relevant and, sometimes anxious to exclude, or even destroy, some which are so highly relevant that they may destroy their case. Always ask to see all the available documentation. You can then decide what is necessary for the preparation and the trial.

Moreover, when they first come to hand, they are unlikely to be in date order. Your first task must be to remedy this. Not only does this assist your initial understanding, but it is the only way in which you can detect those which may be missing.

If one of the witnesses appears to be more vital to the proof of your opponents case, leave him to call the witness. You can thus cross-examine rather than examine him and are not bound by his answers.

The client should now be seen again for two purposes; the first, to enable him to assist you in filling in any lacunae which may have become apparent in the story which he has told you, in the evidence which is by then available, or as a result of the reply which has been received from the opposing party; the second, to give the client an opportunity of explaining or reconciling any variation between his version and that given by the witnesses or disclosed by the documents on discovery.

Assessing the Opponent's Case

You must, as soon as possible, and certainly before discovery in a civil case, or conducting a preliminary enquiry in a criminal case, learn as much as you can ascertain of the case you will have to meet.

It is wise, at one or other of the stages involved in collecting evidence, and, for preference, at an early stage, to invite the client to tell you his views as to the likely case to be presented by his opponent, since he is far more likely to know this than anyone else. Probe for this by questioning the client as to statements which may have been made by his opponent, or those concerned with his opponent during the time when the events occurred giving rise to the litigation. From this you can, yourself, endeavour to assess the likely course which the opposing case will follow. In the same way, it may be possible to anticipate who may be called as witnesses against the client and facilitate further inquiries to form the basis for subsequent cross-examination.

Your task, therefore, at this stage of the matter, is to ascertain the greatest possible amount of information about your own and your opponent's cases, while at the same time endeavouring so far as possible, to tie your opponent down to the precise issues and allegations upon which he may be made to rely. As an aid to the achievement of these objectives, do not forget the importance of asking for further and better particulars of pleadings in civil matters. Additionally, seek further discovery, administer interrogatories and employ all the other aids to investigation.

From this point, there are some differences between the conduct of civil proceedings and the conduct of criminal proceedings.

Discovery of documents

A most import step in civil proceedings is discovery. Far too little attention is paid, in my view, to the importance of discovery as an aid to the technique of persuasion. Too often I find that young or inexperienced clerks or others are sent to carry out a perfunctory examination of the documents produced by the other side. Yet discovery is something which should be undertaken—and particularly is this true of inspection—by, and only by, someone familiar with every aspect of the case, the facts, the law, the issues and the tactics; only in this way can one become thoroughly familiar with the significance of the documents disclosed. It is a well known and most useful routine, in the actual presentation of a case as an advocate in court, to make sure whenever a document is produced as an exhibit that you inspect it, not only in regard to the matter upon which it is adduced in evidence but to see whether any information can be gleaned from it or, for example, from any other pages of a book in which it is contained. Sometimes the lack of continuity of entries in an account book will enable the reliability of the book as a whole to be challenged, and thus cast doubt upon the reliability of the entry upon which the party producing it relies. The record of some transaction which has been overlooked, or the importance of which is not appreciated, may be noted and could be the subject of subsequent inquiries, forming the basis, later, of fruitful cross-examination.

I remember, many years ago, taking part in the long preliminary hearing of an alleged "long-firm fraud." A particular trader had been subpoenaed by the prosecution as a witness to produce his books. These purported to show the price at which the accused was alleged to have purchased large quantities of goods, for which the accused asserted he had, in fact, paid a different price. A request was made to the court for the evidence of this witness to be adjourned and for the books to be delivered to the defence to enable them to be examined. This was done, and the books were then seen by an accountant who gave a report upon them. When the witness resumed his evidence a series of carefully chosen but apparently innocuous questions were put to him concerning various records and entries in the books which were unconnected with the case in question. Questions were pursued despite repeated objections that they did not appear to be relevant to the matter before the court. A subsequent witness for the prosecution was the first witness's partner. He was cross-examined about the entries upon the basis of the accountant's report, and was horrified to find what the books revealed. The key to this had been the manifest inaccuracy in the arithmetic contained in many of the accounts and a number of alterations which appeared to have been made in them. The outcome was not merely the dissolution of partnership between the two witnesses, but the books, being shown to be equally valueless as to the entries on which the prosecution sought to rely, made a valuable contribution not to the proof of the prosecution's case, but towards the ultimate refusal of the court to send the accused for trial.

This same technique needs to be employed wherever possible in the conduct of an investigation for the purposes of discovery. In some cases the remaining entries in a book will have been covered over with the permission of the court. This, of course, renders such a pursuit impossible, but there are many other cases where such a policy can be pursued, and the greatest possible benefit can accrue in the presentation of a case if this aspect of discovery is given close attention.

Expert witnesses

If there is a medical or scientific facet to the case, obtain medical or scientific reports at the earliest possible point of time; in a murder charge, obtain from the Coroner's officer a copy of the pathologist's report on the autopsy, which enables you to decide whether a post-mortem should be arranged by an independent pathologist, and often provides at an early stage much other useful information.

In legal aid cases you may be uncertain whether the expense of obtaining expert opinion or calling expert witnesses will be allowed by the Taxing officer, and, if allowed, at the amount which the expert will require as his fee. You can now obtain authority in advance from the Legal Aid Board in both Civil and Criminal causes. It may be thought indefensible that this decision is not left to responsible lawyer to decide, in relation to the best presentation of their client's case. It may be important, therefore, not to allow these gentlemen, however helpful they may believe themselves to be, to usurp your function. You are in control of your own case and have the sole responsibility for conducting it, and even if, exceptionally, they are unwilling to authorise an expert you may sometimes feel constrained to take the risk, and hope to justify your decision later on taxation, although you will hesitate before flying in the face of a refusal by the Board. As to where the responsibility would lie, in those circumstances, *vis-à-vis* the client, where a witness who should have been called, is not so called, remains to be decided. In most cases, however, no difficulty of this sort is likely to arise.

In claims for personal injuries—whichever side you may represent—write at once for copies of the police and medical reports.

Information as to Client's Background

It is true of most pursuits that the value which comes out of any given situation or subject is in direct relation to the amount that you put into it. Too often one reads reports provided by doctors or other experts which afford insufficient assistance, reflecting the fact that inadequate information has been made available to the doctor or other expert. As previously indicated, a trial is concerned with establishing particular issues. When seeking the assistance of medical or scientific witnesses, do provide them with as much information as you can. Thus, if you are concerned with a case in which the client may be subject to psychiatric or psychological inquiry, collect from him the whole of his background information. Commence by taking him through his life from his earliest recollection. Ascertain all you can about his family, their illnesses, those of his brothers and sisters (which the ultimate medical report will probably call siblings), including whether any of them have been the subject of mental troubles. Indeed, in time you will be able to ask him substantially the same questions as the psychiatrist will put to him.

Instructing the Expert

In a similar fashion in relation to other medical matters, be they in relation to matrimonial problems, personal problems or those of any other medical character, elicit all the information which might be of help to the doctor and see that all of it is forwarded to him.

In scientific matters, make sure that all possible data is available. If you lack previous experience, it is prudent to telephone to the scientist whom you propose to consult and inquire of him what will most assist him to reach a conclusion. For example, if you are seeking to obtain a report on handwriting from an expert on questioned documents, it is no use sending him a questioned signature and a single example of the genuine signature. He will certainly want a number of examples of the latter and, if there is more than one possible forgery involved, as many examples of forgery as possible.

In addition to this, you should bear in mind that a scientist or a doctor giving an expert opinion will generally only view the problem from the angle at which it is put to him, and is only likely to answer the questions which you have posed. To this end it is desirable to raise specifically for his consideration points which you seek to establish in the presentation of the case, in order to canvass his views as to the value that should be placed on such theories.

Be anxious to explain to the doctor the purpose for which he has been asked to see the client; and set down the particular issues and allegations which are made on one side or the other which it is desired, if possible, to establish or refute.

If, in the process, you have formed any ideas of your own which indicate possible lines of inquiry, set these down and invite the doctor to state whether, as a matter of medical knowledge, such assumptions or inferences are wrong; and, if so, where and why. The function of an expert witness is to give opinion evidence on the basis of ascertained facts. Often his evidence proceeds on no more than a series of hypotheses, some of which may be more probable than others. Make sure, therefore, that you provide him with as much of the surrounding circumstances as you can, including witnesses proofs and statements.

Thus, a pathologist's opinion that a head injury "was consistent with" a blow with a blunt instrument may be qualified if he is told that the deceased was found lying head first along the bottom of a flight of stairs. Finally if, when you receive the report, there are parts which either you do not clearly understand or you believe should be the subject of further inquiry and discussion, either speak to the doctor or scientist about it on the telephone or ask for an appointment to see him.

Question him until you clearly understand what is truly involved, and pick his brains as to the contrary view which may be presented by experts called by your opponent.

It must, of course, be appreciated that I only advocate that this should be done at the point at which one is investigating the basis for presentation of the case. I do not suggest, in an ordinary personal accident case where one is asking for an initial medical report, that one should do more than ask for the report. Very often, however, it is upon the basis of that report that one raises the further comments and inquiries. Moreover, where the client is already under the care of a private practitioner, arrangements for him to attend the consultant of your nomination should only be made after securing the agreement of the general practitioner, or by asking him to arrange an appointment and tactfully suggesting, in passing, the consultant's name. Most doctors, you will find, welcome such suggestions.

Form of Medical Report

It is important to ensure when you receive the report that it is, as far as possible, prepared in such a way as renders it most useful for production in court. I suggest that a medical report should be sub-divided into three parts, and should always be accompanied by a separate document intended to assist the legal advisers of the patient. At the outset it should contain the name and address of the patient, particulars of the symptoms from which he has been suffering, particulars of the treatment, if any, to which he was subjected by the doctor, and any similar facts—which should be set down in chronological order and, if in technical language, with non-technical explanatory language in parenthesis. Next the report should postulate questions which the doctor sees it as his task to answer. This affords two advantages. It enables the recipient of the report to satisfy himself that the premises upon which the doctor's conclusion is based are accurate and comprehensive. Secondly it enables the doctor, in considering the matter, to pinpoint additional information which he requires to ensure that he has all available data.

The last part of the report should then give the doctor's opinions and conclusions together with the prognosis and further suggestions for treatment, if any.

The letter to accompany the report should be quite distinct and separate and should contain any suggestions which the doctor has to make as to the better presentation of the patient's case, together with any suggestions for further investigations or inquiries, and lastly any guidance which can be given as to dangers which may lurk, at present undetected, but which might be known to the other side and become the subject of attack by them. The purpose in keeping this covering letter separate from the report is so that, in the event of an order being made for exchange of medical reports (and it seems likely that the exchanging of information between doctors will increase rather than diminish) technical guidance on the conduct of your case or weaknesses which may present themselves should not be the subject of disclosure to your opponents. There is no requirement in practice or in law that information of this nature be made available to your opponents.

Familiarise yourself with recent procedural changes which now make the exchanging of experts reports compulsory.

Medicine, Science and the Law

Do not proceed on the assumption that, because doctors, scientists and lawyers have trained minds, they necessarily think alike. In the British Academy of Forensic Sciences, with which I have been concerned, we bring together medicine, science and the law. It has seemed to me that the differences between each of these disciplines are well illustrated by their reaction to the procedure of a trial at law. The scientist, trained in the belief that the pursuit of truth is the most vital, believes that everything known to him should be given in evidence. The doctor, trained within the framework of the Hippocratic oath, considers that all which comes to his knowledge in the pursuit of his vocation is secret, and that nothing should be revealed in evidence which can possibly be withheld. The lawyer takes a third point of view and believes—or, more correctly, hopes—that, so far as possible, only that should be revealed which supports his case. To some extent none of them is wrong and, within the framework of their own discipline, all of them are right although not within the context of the law. A trial at law does not in fact involve the pursuit of the whole truth. In saying this, I must not be taken as suggesting that a trial at law is a contest to decide who can tell the greatest lies, although this may sometimes seem to be the case. The true position is, perhaps, best illuminated by an example which I have used on other occasions.

Assume that the question for determination is whether a particular bacillus or germ which we shall name X is the cause of cancer. Such a contention might well be examined by a scientist in the process of research; by a doctor in his endeavours to restore a patient to health, and by a lawyer as part of an allegation in a case with which he might be concerned. The doctor and the scientist can only fully achieve their objective if they can positively decide whether or not X is the culprit; they must search for the truth whilst examining every facet of the contention. A trial at law, however, is not a quest for truth in this sense. Such a trial depends upon the making of certain allegations or assertions by the one side and the refutation of them by the other; it is concerned to inquire whether or not those asertions or allegations have been established or refuted in accordance with the principles of evidence which are applicable. Thus, in a criminal trial, the question is whether the prosecution has proved beyond reasonable doubt, and in a civil trial whether it has been established on a balance of probabilities, that X is the cause of cancer. Whilst, therefore, the doctor and the scientist are engaged in an inquisitorial pursuit in which they are seeking the truth, the lawyer is engaged in an accusatorial pursuit to see whether a limited onus of proof has been discharged. When doctors inquire into whether X is the cause of cancer they must investigate at the same time ancillary questions, namely, if X is not the cause of cancer, what then is the cause of it. It is small consolation for the scientist or the doctor to say to the ailing person, "you will be happy to know that I am satisfied that X, which is within your body, is not the cause of cancer, but nevertheless you have cancer and I cannot tell you what is causing it." By comparison, however, the lawyer deals with a different situation. He is concerned only to prove or disprove the particular allegation. It is no part of the function of the court to extend the inquiry whether X is the cause of cancer so as to discover what in fact is the cause; if the court acquits A of the murder of X, it has no duty to ascertain in addition who in fact murdered X; although it is beyond dispute that if it is possible to prove that Y was in fact the sole murderer this must, in the process, necessarily eliminate A. It is not suprising, in the circumstances, that the doctor (and for that matter the scientist) becomes utterly confused when called to give evidence. At the point when he proposes to reveal his most striking discovery, someone pops up and tells him "No, Doctor Jones, we can't have that." At still another point in the trial when he is expressing an opinion based upon his findings, which incidentally he has pursued with the best possible goodwill to all mankind, another gentleman pops up and proceeds to put to him a series of questions, which the doctor often considers rude and insulting in so much as they seem designed to show that all his work was really a waste of time. Much, however, of the misunderstanding between the two professions might be eliminated if there were a better appreciation by each that the objective which the one and the other are pursuing is not the same.

Cross-examination of Medical Witnesses

The fact remains, however, that expert witnesses in general, and medical witnesses in particular, provide, if the advocate is properly prepared, the most useful and easily assailable material for successful cross-examination. Witnesses as to facts speak to matters of positive recollection within their own experience. There may be wide divergencies between different witnesses of fact as to what occurred at a given time, but having once reached a conclusion as to their recollection they are pre-disposed to cling to, and refuse to resile from, the version to which they have committed themselves. Precluded from expressing opinions, they must rely only on their memory of the events, inadequate as that may be. Doctors, by comparison, are dealing, within the realm of informed opinion, with the subject-matter of an art, which is neither exact nor necessarily scientific. Their difficulty is best illustrated by an example which was of daily occurrence before the passing of the Road Safety Act 1967.

A doctor gives evidence that he examined an accused person on a certain day. He describes the examination which he conducted and asserts that, in his opinion, the defendant's ability to drive a motor vehicle was impaired through drink. He is shown the results of an analysis of urine which certifies that the alcoholic content of the urine was equivalent to 140 milligrams of alcohol to 100 millilitres of blood, and opines that this corroborates the view which he found on the examination.

Under cross-examination it can often be demonstrated that nearly all the clinical symptoms on which he relies, taken individually, can be explained in terms other than those of insobriety. The slurred speech and unsteady gait may be the normal speech and the way of walking of the accused, whom the doctor had not previously seen. The bounding pulse may be occasioned by a neurotic state accelerated by his being under arrest. Nystagmus—which means no more than an involuntary oscillatory movement of the eyeball—may have been caused by an ear disease of which the doctor was uninformed. Even the smell of drink on his breath may, the doctor has to agree, possibly have been occasioned by one large sherry, the smell of which is particularly potent. Thus the doctor is thrown back on the riposte— often made with some feeling—that taking each symptom individually is unsatisfactory; that his view was formed on the basis of the symptoms as a whole, now fortified by the urine content. Finally, he can be forced to concede that the British Medical Association is correct that one urine specimen, which alone was available, is unreliable; that the value of the analysis depends upon whether the urine had been in the bladder for less or more than two hours, a fact which is not known to him, and that 140 milligrams to 100 millilitres in the blood is a borderline case between sobriety and insobriety.

The doctor may be professionally convinced that the accused was unfit to drive; with such concessions in cross-examination, however, would any jury of laymen be likely to convict? And if they acquit the doctor may feel aggrieved—not at the acquittal, but at what he regards as an attack upon his professional competence.

Choice of Doctor

How then are you to know the best doctors to whom you might have your clients referred? The process by which an intelligent solicitor ascertains an appropriate doctor is not necessarily the same as the process by which an intelligent client chooses his solicitor or an intelligent solicitor in turn chooses a competent counsel. A ready source of information are the universities and the teaching hospitals. I particularly mention the teaching hospitals in preference to other types of hospital because they have tended to attract to themselves the most experienced and able consultant physicians and surgeons, although in recent years there has been a greater tendency for wider dispersal of ability and experience. This is not to decry the ability of those who do not reach a teaching hospital; all doctors cannot be so appointed. If your locality is not served by a teaching hospital, an inquiry at the hospital local to your area may be the means of ascertaining who is most skilled and experienced in the particular speciality. Note the words "most skilled and experienced in the particular speciality." Whoever gives evidence in a court of law as a medical expert must, at the outset of his evidence, qualify himself as an expert. "Qualifying" is a term of art and means not more than this: the law of evidence does not always permit, under the hearsay rules, the reciting of facts which are not directly relevant to the issue before the court. For example, what happened in a set of circumstances similar to those with which the court is concerned is not generally regarded as being germane to the determination of what occurred in the particular case under inquiry. Nevertheless, an expert witness may often need to refer to such cases to show the basis upon which he reached his conclusions. Over and above this no witness, other than an expert, is allowed to express opinions. He must limit himself to facts. Thirdly, and finally on this aspect, the mere fact that a witness is a registered medical practitioner (which incidentally is the correct legal description for a doctor which you should use in the introductory questions as to his qualifications, when calling a doctor as a witness) does not qualify him as an expert upon every aspect of medicine and surgery, any more than the fact that a person is qualified as a solicitor or barrister necessarily constitutes him an expert on private international or admiralty law or practice. It is, thus, essential at the outset of his evidence that the expert satisfy the court that by virtue of his special training and experience in a special field he is qualified as an expert to deal with the particular matters with which the court is there and then concerned. Expertise need not, however, depend on professional or academic qualifications. In one case concerning the proper methods of applying splints to damaged limbs, the court expressed a marked preference for the evidence of a medical orderly to that of highly qualified doctors, in the academic sense, who had been called as witnesses at the hearing, because he had extensively applied splints in the field during the war.

It is important, therefore, to ascertain the precise qualification of any doctor you may intend to call as a witness, and to inquire closely into, and record, his experience with the particular problem under investigation. The extent of his research, the breadth of his active experience, the celebrated doctors with whom he has worked, his contribution to medical literature and journals on the subject—all these matters are as important, if not more important, than the fact that he is a Fellow of a Royal College.

However, when you find the particular doctor whom you would like to call, he may be unwilling or uncooperative about giving evidence. Many doctors, understandably, take the view that their function is to relieve sickness and that time is not best occupied kicking heels around courts waiting for cases to be heard. Others, for reasons I have already touched upon, are loath to be drawn into the contentious atmosphere of a court and subjected to cross-examination aimed at diminishing their reputation as skilled practitioners. Still others, whilst willing to give evidence, are singularly inarticulate in the witness box and may, as a result, do your case infinitely more harm than good. Quite the best kind of expert, and they are unfortunately anything but thick upon the ground, and as a result anything but thick in the witness box, are those who have devoted time and study to their subject, have a wide experience in it, understand the purpose of a trial at law, have experience of giving evidence and, above all, are clearly apprised of their own limitations. If you fail to obtain the necessary assistance from the universities or the hospitals, you may have recourse to the British Academy of Forensic Sciences, one of the objects of which is to ensure that expert witnesses of standing and integrity are available and that information is afforded as to the best available expert witness in any particular field. By taking an interest in the meetings organised by the Academy, by studying its journal, *Medicine, Science* and the Law, or by attending medico-legal societies or similar bodies you will gather, over the years, a sufficient knowledge of the elements of forensic medicine and science and the identity of those particularly skilled in the forensic medicine and science to enable you, of your own knowledge, to choose those best suited to serve the interests of your client. The willingness of the expert to devote the necessary time to your case may be a vital consideration. Wherever possible it is desirable that he should sit throughout the hearing of the case; that you should call him as late in the proceedings as the procedure permits, so that he is familiar with the evidence advanced and the counter arguments and hypotheses, and that he remains available to advise at every stage. An expert witness, unlike others, is always permitted to remain in court during the whole proceedings.

The preliminary inquiry

In the conduct of a criminal defence, particularly one going for trial, I cannot too strongly stress the importance of a proper regard for the preliminary inquiry. In relation to the trial of a criminal cause on indictment, the preliminary inquiry is an important aspect of discovery. The Criminal Justice Act which was passed in 1967* introduced a number of useful time-saving devices in regard to the preliminary inquiry, but unless the present and next generation of lawyers continues to use the preliminary inquiry to its best advantage, there is a real risk that it will die and disappear. Already, ominous arguments have been advanced to this end, and an increasing tendency to avoid using the procedure is speeding its demise. By reason of this Act, it is no longer essential for the witnesses for the prosecution to attend the preliminary hearing and give their evidence so that it can be written down by the clerk in the form of a deposition. The preliminary procedure may now take one of three forms. Statements of the prosecution witnesses may be served upon the defence. A represented defendant may then concur in a formal committal without any consideration of evidence whatsoever; he may require some of the witnesses to attend for the purpose of giving evidence so

* Now contained in Magistrates Courts Act 1980 (see s.6(2)).

that he may cross-examine them, or he may require a full preliminary inquiry in accordance with section 6(1) of the Magistrates' Courts Act 1980. Although the lawyer needs to exercise the greatest possible diligence and care in the investigation of the case with which he is concerned, it is regrettably the fact that, with the present pressure of work and shortages of staff, there is an increasing tendency to take the line of least resistance and either to agree to a formal committal for trial or not to have the witnesses brought to court at all. There are some cases where it will be quite clear that the client is guilty; that the prosecution can prove its case and will not reduce the charges, and where all that remains is an address in mitigation. There will be many cases in which it will be quite unnecessary to require all the witnesses to be present. In a significant number of cases, however, it will be desirable, and in the author's opinion, essential, to select particular witnesses whose attendance should be required at a preliminary hearing.

Importance of the Preliminary Inquiry

Some years ago a Committee which sat under the chairmanship of Mr. Justice Byrne, one of the outstanding criminal lawyers of his time, stated specifically; "We would like to emphasise that it is our unanimous opinion that in taking preliminary inquiries justices and their clerks are performing a duty as important and valuable as any other they are called upon to perform."

In a Memorandum of February 1964, the Council of the Law Society stressed the advantages of taking depositions; a view from which it has never resiled.

Subsequent experience has more than justified the views of the Law Society. The predictable tendency of advocates to dispense with a preliminary inquiry has done nothing to improve the administration of justice. The absence of an opportunity for the lower court and the opposing advocates to scrutinise the evidence has resulted in many cases being committed for trial which should have been dismissed at a preliminary inquiry. Trials have been lengthened and time wasted due to the muddled and confused state of statements and exhibits, and counts have been included in indictments which a proper inquiry in the magistrates' court would have eliminated.

The strongest argument which can be used against the continuation of the preliminary inquiry is that the average practitioner does not employ it to the best advantage; others, although present at the inquiry, appear barely to employ it at all. Indeed, a pamphlet by two barristers asserted one of the "golden rules of the Bar" to be "ask no questions at committal proceedings." If it exists, it is a rule of gold which fails the acid test. One has only to remember the cases of Stephen Ward, Bodkin Adams, the Moors case, the Thorpe case and many others to realise that such a golden rule is honoured more in the breach than in the observance. It is a rule which needs to be observed only by those who are unfamiliar with their case, and lack the skill and ability to cross-examine with discretion. It is true that the inexperienced advocate may, in inadvertence or ignorance, reveal weaknesses in the prosecution case, which the prosecution can remedy by serving notice of additional evidence, or otherwise rectify at the trial. That this may occur is not to be taken as an indication that the preliminary inquiry should be rarely required or fully utilised; at best, it demonstrates the need to watch experienced advocates conducting such inquiries before yourself embarking upon the conduct of them. My objective is necessarily to demonstrate how it should be best employed with experience, and not how it can be made dangerous by incompetence. If, however, you never attempt it, you will always remain inexperienced.

The preliminary inquiry enables evidence to be subjected to objection on the ground of inadmissibility, including that it is irrelevant and unduly prejudicial. Moreover, written statements which are not subjected to scrutiny and cross-examination often harbour concealed dangers. There is a certain technique involved in the preparing of proofs of evidence and, for fear that it should be misconstrued as an attack upon police officers, let it be said that it is a measure of abuse as much available to the defence as to those concerned with the prosecution. It is, however, of less importance when pursued by the defence since this cannot result in the wrongful detention of an innocent person. Despite the high incidence of crime it will be a sorry day for England if the protection of the innocent ever takes second place to the conviction of the guilty. This technique of statement taking, which is also found at the heart of successful cross-examination, is the ability by suggestion to implant into the mind of a witness or potential witness some belief as to facts which he henceforward adopts as his own recollection. The existence of this technique needs to be borne in mind whenever it is necessary to peruse and consider statements coming from the opposing side and not merely in relation to committal proceedings. Take a simple example: A body is found which, according to the pathologist's report, indicates the death occurred as a result of an assault which took place at about eight o'clock on a particular evening. X is under suspicion as the assailant. Some weeks later a statement is being taken from a witness who ultimately says that he saw the assailant in the vicinity of the crime on the day in question but that he cannot remember the time. Is it likely, in these circumstances, that his proof of evidence will emerge indicative of that uncertain state of mind? What in fact occurs is that he is told what the pathologist has said, which implants in his mind the possibility that it must have been 8 p.m. A series of questions are then put to him designed to show that, from his own movements on that day, he might personally have observed X at 8 p.m. because that is the time he returns from his work and when he would have been in the vicinity. Nowhere will it appear in the statement that he could similarly have observed X and been in the vicinity at eight o'clock in the morning when he was going to work. In the result, all the probabilities are that his statement, when presented to the defence, would simply read: "At about eight o'clock in the evening on August 3 last I observed X walking along Watling Street in the direction of the Three Feathers public house."

Testing the Truth of Statements

Commonplace in the taking of statements, this technique establishes the first justification for preserving the preliminary hearing, namely that it enables the defence, in the absence of the jury, to test the circumstances under which statements were taken; whether, for example, the witness was certain from the outset as to the time when he had seen X and, indeed, as to the actual day when he saw him; and whether, moreover, it was necessarily X whom he saw. Those who would abolish the preliminary hearing then question the need to do this at a preliminary hearing. "Why," they ask, "not do it at the trial? If the witness is unreliable that is surely the place to demonstrate it by cross-examination?" The fallacy of this argument is self-evident. A jury is composed of laymen; the psychological effect of evidence unsuccessfully probed before them involves the risk that they will place an utterly disproportionate value upon the fact that the defence had baselessly challenged a prosecution witness, who had emerged from it unscathed. It is not for nothing that generations of advocates have been wisely taught never to ask a question at a trial to which they do not know the answer, although no one suggests this precept can or must universally be followed. Whilst this largely remains true at committal proceedings, it is often wiser to take the risk involved at that stage in order to protect your flanks later.

It is true that sometimes in the past little or no cross-examination has taken place at the preliminary hearing, fostered by the belief that it is disadvantageous for the defence to show its hand before the trial. If an advocate is able only to cross-examine at a preliminary hearing in such manner as reveals the defence, then he should adopt one of two courses—either spend time in the courts watching the way it is done by experienced practitioners, or give up advocacy. In experienced hands the preliminary inquiry can be conducted so that the deposition provides a signpost to the advocate at the trials as to which questions should and which should not be put to the witnesses; it can lay the foundation for the tactical conduct of the proceedings; and it may relieve the accused of the hardship of going for trial. In any case, the good defence of an innocent person rarely suffers from early disclosure; only the guilty, with a bad or no defence, need fear its early revelation. Those who counsel that advocates should reserve cross-examination for the trial itself, often overlook the fact that should a witness die or become unfit to attend at the trial, his deposition taken at the committal proceedings may be adduced in evidence. This is because the accused had been afforded the opportunity to cross-examine at the preliminary hearing. An advocate who had declined the opportunity to do so, might thus live to regret it.

Indeed in many cases the disclosure of the line of defence, which will later fully emerge, is a shield for, rather than a weapon against, his client. This is especially true of a bona fide alibi defence which must now be notified to the prosecution, since it enables its reliability to be tested. If it cannot be broken or weakened, it can only be strengthened.

In the second place, acceptance of a mere statement, in place of a sworn deposition which is subject to cross-examination, pre-supposes that whoever takes the statement has elicited every possible fact and lead which the witness is capable of providing. It needs to be remembered that the first stage in a prosecution for crime is that the police endeavour to ascertain who may have committed it. Once done, the whole character of the investigation changes; by the time the point is reached at which proofs of evidence are prepared, the prosecution are no longer concerned to uncover evidence which will indicate which of an unknown number of persons may have committed the crime, but are necessarily directing their attention to the presentation of evidence to prove that the suspect is the person who committed it. Even were this not so, it is asking the impossible to expect the most honest and competent police officer to hope to elicit, in any statement he may take, facts which might be of assistance to the defence since, until he knows precisely what is the defence and what principles of law are applicable, he cannot know for what information he should look.

Eliciting Further Evidence

Thus emerges the second important aspect of cross-examination of witnesses in preliminary hearings, namely the probing for, and eliciting of, data, facts and leads which may enable those preparing the defence to unearth facts or witnesses who would not otherwise be available. Those who, somewhat naively, ask, "Why then cannot this be done at the trial?" should be asked, in turn, whether anyone with experience of a trial on indictment really believes that a High Court judge, circuit judge or recorder would allow defending counsel to occupy the time of the court in probing for possible lines of inquiry. Within minutes counsel would be faced with the penetrating question "Pray tell me, Mr. A., where is all this getting us?" Indeed, were the truthful answer given, it could serve no purpose other than the basis for a Bateman cartoon. Moreover, once the trial has commenced there is neither time nor opportunity, in most cases, to pursue further inquiries. Thus, in the earlier example, the witness would be cross-examined as to who else may have been present at the time when he believes he saw X on August 3. If others were in the neighbourhood, he might provide just sufficient information to enable them to be traced. Moreover, if X's defence is that he was in the vicinity at 8 a.m. and not 8 p.m., facts descriptive of the circumstances then prevailing might be elicited to confirm X's story; and in either instance, given time before trial, corroborative evidence might be obtained. All of this is generally impossible on written statements alone, although the prosecution will have had weeks or months in preparation to follow every possible lead.

Testing the Client's Case

In the third place—and this is especially something of which few, other than lawyers, appear to have either knowledge or understanding—a vital part of the presentation of the defence often involves the protection of a client against himself. It is essential in any satisfactory system of justice, particularly where, as in England, the onus rests upon the prosecution, that all, from the innocent to the meanest criminal, should be legally represented if they so desire. Professional ethics rightly dictate that neither barristers nor solicitors should present as innocent those who have admitted their guilt to them; the most they may do, in those circumstances, is to put the prosecution to proof of the case against their client. Accordingly, no defending advocate worth his salt ever privately puts the direct question to the client "Are you guilty of this offence?" Nevertheless, it is essential in the interests of the client, once he has given his explanation, that a competent lawyer should endeavour to evaluate, in the client's interest, both the reliability of his version of the facts and the likelihood of the Crown failing to satisfy a jury. If the lawyer is dissatisfied as to the probability of either he may endeavour to persuade the client to plead guilty; that the jury will undoubtedly find him guilty and that his best interests may be served in some way other than a contest. Thus the cross-examination at the preliminary inquiry enables the informed advocate to test any part of the story given to him by the client, of which he has doubt, against the account of the prosecution witnesses given under cross-examination. Prior to this, any attempt to convince the client of the impossibility of his position and the strength of the evidence of the prosecution witnesses is frequently met with the argument, "They are lying—you wait until they are cross-examined." Moreover, to tender advice to a client which precludes the presentation of his defence to an independent tribunal, based on untested written statements alone, might well amount to negligence.

Reduction of Charges

The next important use to which the preliminary inquiry should be put (and which cannot be achieved by mere delivery of statements) is—apart from the possibility of avoiding the trial in its entirety—to facilitate the reduction of the charges and issues at the ultimate trial and to take the sting out of what might otherwise be presented as a far more serious case. Again an actual example may illustrate. A professional man is charged at the magistrates' court with two different classes of offence, namely forgery and making false statements in tax returns. It is hardly necessary to stress the difference in magnitude as between these allegations. Upon the basis of statements obtained by the Inland Revenue, both these charges are believed (erroneously) to be justified. As a result of cross-examination in the magistrates' court it is rendered plain that the first charge could not possibly be sustained. A submission of no case to answer on this charge is wrongly rejected. However, when the indictment arrives the prosecution have abandoned forgery and accept a plea of guilty to the lesser charges. Thus considerable anguish is saved the defendant; an inevitable contest at the trial on this issue is avoided; a reduced penalty is assured; and expense and effort are saved which must otherwise have been incurred had the prosecution been able to persist in the charge of forgery.

Inconsistent Statements

Another of the virtues of employing the procedure is that any subsequent deviation by the witness from his sworn deposition may be put to him at the subsequent trial. This is no mere technical gimmick or stratagem since weeks may elapse, in a substantial case, between the preliminary hearing and the trial; and months may have elapsed between his initial statement to the police and his ultimate evidence. It is proper that there should be put to a witness inconsistent statements which he has previously made on oath, but the value of this check is diminished if he is able to say (as a convenient escape), "I did not swear that on oath. I was merely giving information to the police as best I could and may have been mistaken."

Benefits to the Prosecution

Are, then, all the advantages of a preliminary inquiry available only for the defence? Indeed not. It frequently happens as a result of the preliminary inquiry and cross-examination, that a weakness in the prosecution case becomes manifest. This may be supplemented by additional evidence. It often emerges that the form in which the case has been presented is misconceived, which enables different charges to be framed in the indictment. Just as witnesses may come forward as a result of the preliminary hearing to assist the defence, they have been known to come forward to assist the prosecution. It often contributes to a decision to enter a plea of guilty. A significant part of the congestion in the higher courts stems from the failure of prosecutors, since the passing of the Criminal Justice Act 1967, to avail themselves of the committal proceedings to check the strength and completeness of their case.

Effect on the Trial Itself

The judge has an important part to play in an English criminal trial. Although the jury are said to be the sole judges of fact, this has never prevented judges expressing their own opinions, and their summing-up unquestionably has a significant effect upon the minds of juries. Judges, however, being only human, are likely to be influenced by innumerable factors; some form an opinion about a case in the early stages. The judge is enabled to see the depositions and the indictment before a case

41

commences, before even the jury have heard what the case is about. The course of many trials may well have been affected by judicious cross-examination in the magistrates' court; it may provide the judge with a wholly different slant upon the case for the prosecution as revealed from the initial evidence of the witnesses. Moreover, effective cross-examination, as already demonstrated in a different context, will often convince the prosecution of the weakness of its case and facilitate acceptance of a plea to a lesser charge. To take another actual example, a youth from a good home was charged with the serious criminal offence of possessing a firearm with intent to endanger life. As a result of the cross-examination at the preliminary hearing the matter was disposed of, at the stage of indictment, by acceptance of a plea to common assault (on the technical basis that he pointed the weapon, without intending to fire it), warranting no more than probation. There can be no question but that such a result could never have been achieved without a full trial had the defence only had available to them the proofs of evidence of prosecution witnesses which had not been tested in cross-examination.

It was, in the author's opinion, exceedingly unfortunate that a Divisional Court in 1973* expressed opinions (which were *obiter*) designed to restrict the compass of committal proceedings. They were not to be used, they opined, as a rehearsal for the trial. Committal proceedings however, are the creation of statute, and there is no provision which precludes any of the aids to the achievement of justice which are outlined above.

The situation, in my opinion, has been made worse by the passage of the Criminal Justice Act 1987, which adopted some of the recommendations of the Fraud Trials Committee. As a result, if certain authorities, namely the Directors of Public Prosecutions or of the Serious Fraud Office, the Commissioners of Inland Revenue or of Customs and Excise or the Secretary of State himself, are of the opinion that there is sufficient evidence for the person charged to be committed for trial in a case of fraud which they consider is of such seriousness and complexity that it is appropriate that the management of the case should be taken over by the

* R. v. *Epping and Harlow Justices, ex p. Massaro* [1973] 1 All E.R. 1011.

Crown Court without delay, the function of the committing magistrates ceases forthwith, and the accused is sent at once for trial. Thus, in those cases where the need to sift the evidence and give the accused the fullest opportunity to learn precisely the case he has to meet is most needed, both those desirable objectives are wholly frustrated. In those very cases where, because of their "seriousness and complexity" they have been investigated, at their leisure, by the police with the help of the appropriate authority, over very many months, and often longer, with the fullest opportunity to scrutinise the innumerable documents, the accused faces trial, deprived of the protection and benefit of committal proceedings. What is as bad, and indeed, perhaps, worse, is that the jurisdiction of an independent court is ousted and the decision taken by the prosecutor himself.

Moreover, the Act expressly provides that the "designated authority's decision to give notice of transfer" (by which means the procedure is invoked) "shall not be subject to appeal or liable to be questioned in any court."

The Fraud Trials Committee advanced a number of reasons for recommending this procedure, none of which bear real examination. The first, because of the length and delay of committal proceedings, which, additionally enable fraudsters to continue their operations to the detriment of the public. In fact, the new procedure far from shortening the time involved, manifestly lengthens it. Months now pass, as witness the recent Guiness trial, over which repeated applications are made, and arguments ensue, before the trial judge, generally in chambers which thus goes unreported, often to the bewilderment of those who know of the applications but remain uninformed as to what transpired. Since by then the businesses involved usually have collapsed, or the accused removed from them, it is hardly correct to suggest that the public suffer. The second reason given was "abuse," namely that the accused use committal proceedings as a means of examining prosecution witnesses at length, hoping to obtain material to formulate a defence. There cannot, surely, be any other country in the world—certainly not in any part which is to be regarded as civilised—which would describe taking the opportunity to test the veracity and credibility of the prosecution witnesses and learning, in depth, the case raised against you, as being an abuse of the process of justice.

The third reason given by the Committee was the unsatisfactory nature of a tribunal of Lay Magistrates to preside over committal proceedings. There is some merit in this, but the common sense approach is not to abolish the committal procedure but the lay magistrates from this function and substitute stipendiary magistrates who have always performed the function well.

Their fourth reason was "cost." An odd reason in itself when it is observed that the place where the delays now occur, in the crown courts, involve in excess of three times more expense, at least, than in the lower courts, which is greatly increased by the presence of so many silks, juniors and solicitors that the trial often has to be moved into courts of greater cubic capacity.

The last reason was that defendants were rarely discharged in committal proceedings. That studiously avoids recognising their own third reason, and that this derives from the use of untrained laymen to perform the requisite functions. In any event, I have known many cases where the proceedings have resulted in discharge of the accused with great savings of time and money.

Faced, then, with these formidable inroads into the procedures which have hitherto assisted the attainment of justice, what should be the approach of the advocate? If you are prosecuting, and, as such, something of a minister of justice, you must ensure that the defence is afforded the fullest opportunity to familiarise itself with all relevant documents, not only those on which you intend to rely but those which are rejected. Similar considerations apply to witnesses' statements, both those to be used and those discarded. Finally, it behoves you, especially in such fraud cases, to adhere to the highest principles guiding prosecutors in this country, and always to lean in favour of the needs of the defence, where they may be in conflict with what you see as the needs of the prosecution.

If you are defending, you must strive to make good, as far as this may be possible, the deficiencies in procedure, which are otherwise available to you in other types of case. Whilst there may no longer be access to the higher court in regard to the committal, you can have access to it if you are to be deprived of any necessary safeguards or facilities which go to the proper presentation of your client's defence.

Paradoxically, in face of the claim that the new procedure is designed to save time and cost, numerous applications are now made to the presiding judge on matters which hitherto were never the subject of proceedings at all. These may take anything from an hour to a day or more. They usually revolve round procedures to be employed when the evidence is adduced, and the legal research and preparation which you should conduct should be no less or different from that dedicated standard which should be applied to a full-blooded hearing. In accord with a growing tendency, the judges welcome the use of skeletal arguments in written form, and this is particularly so on procedural applications of this nature. Prepare these with care, setting out each point in a numbered paragraph; express your argument clearly and as simply as possible, and, as with all good advocacy, eliminate any surplus which you can manage without. Since, however, unsuccessfully, the procedure is designed to save time, the judges will appreciate any endeavours you may make to achieve this, and since appeal from their interim decisions will necessarily further delay the trial, they will strive to avoid them so far as they are able.

Preparation of witnesses

When you are in possession of all the information about the case which you are likely to acquire, I recommend that you should, if a solicitor, and time permits, bring back your client and the witnesses and subject each of them to the sort of rigorous cross-examination which they are likely to experience in a court of law. This serves a number of purposes and, of course, an experience of practical advocacy in the courts is of enormous assistance in conducting such an inquiry. In the first place it accustoms the witness to the atmosphere he is sometimes likely to encounter in court; a climate which is often more calculated to confuse than clarify; it gives him an indication in answer to the question so often put to solicitors, "What are they likely to ask me?" It tends, moreover, to bring into the open weaknesses in the case so that you have at least an opportunity to find evidence which may support those parts of the story which now seem to require it. It enables you to make sure that the maximum effect is obtained from the combined evidence of your witnesses. Finally, it enables you in some cases to save the client from the consequences of his own lies or over optimistic imagination. Even honest clients may become so imbued with the desire to win that they may unconsciously gild the lily. Your task, where this occurs, is to break down their story and demonstrate its unreliability, thereby showing the wisdom of keeping to the true facts, or, perhaps, of seeking a compromise and thus disposing of the litigation.

I am not for one moment advocating that witnesses should be told what to say or that their evidence or recollection should be corrected the one against the other. This would clearly be both improper and undesirable. For less am I advocating that which is not unknown in the American system under which witnesses are rehearsed and groomed, the attorney taking care to indicate to them which parts of their evidence they should forget and which parts they should add. It is, however, essential that a witness should be fully tested on every aspect of his evidence to ensure, so far as possible, that neither he nor you are taken by surprise at the trial. Great care should be taken to ensure that you merely clarify his mind and do not seek to distort his recollection.

Interviews by Counsel

Currently barristers, unlike solicitors, are only permitted to interview the client and expert witnesses. They must rely on the solicitor to interview the witnesses as to fact. Many facile and colourful arguments are advanced to justify this time-honoured rule. It is said, for example, that the barrister might be prompted to tailor the evidence. It is highly unlikely, however, that the barrister will be more prone to this than the solicitor, and there is something highly devious and hypocritical in winking at the possibility of a solicitor doing it but denying the opportunity to a barrister.

It is then said that even if a witness is rehearsed by a solicitor, the barrister, never having met the witness, will question him afresh in court, without knowledge of what has gone before. This argument deliberately ignores the information which the solicitor might convey in the brief to counsel or in conference. Moreover if it is so undesirable for the barrister to see the witnesses for such questionable and dubious reasons, why allow him to meet and converse with the most vital witness of all, namely the litigant himself? If he can successfully overcome the temptations of Scylla he should be able to avoid the danger of Charybdis.

In fact the bulk of contentious legal business is conducted in the county and magistrates' courts by solicitors who both interview the witnesses and conduct the advocacy without the dire consequences which it is said would flow from the removal of this rule affecting Barristers. In my view, it is outmoded and should be abolished, so that every advocate can see and assess his client's witnesses as he does the client himself. Perhaps there is now a greater possibility of this coming about. Once both branches have equal rights of audience this practice will need urgent review.

Planning Inquiries

It has become the practice on Town and Country Planning Inquiries to hand in typed copies of the proofs of witnesses for the use of the Inspector. This practice has spread to certain other tribunals; and you will be well advised to ascertain in advance if this is expected. It is certainly a practice to be encouraged in all litigous matters.

Where it is, make sure you have sufficient copies for each member of the Tribunal, (an Inspector sits alone in Town Planning Inquiries) for the witness, your opponent and his assistant, and a few spare copies for other interested parties. You are at a disadvantage if you go unprepared and must require the Tribunal to make a note of evidence normally produced typed.

The fact that the evidence will be thus placed on record, underlines the need for careful and accurate preparation employing all the techniques which are elsewhere examined in this book. There will occasionally be cases, but they will be rare, where you consider that oral evidence will be preferable to written, in which case you may insist on that procedure being followed. This could occur where you know that a sharp difference exists between the opposing versions and your witnesses are likely to convey a better impression in evidence if given orally. I stress however that it will seldom occur that this consideration will outweigh the annoyance generated in the Tribunal by forcing it to make a verbatim note.

Preparation for cross-examination

Whether you are a solicitor proposing to submit a brief to counsel, in those cases where you have no right of audience yourself, or whether you are going to conduct the case yourself—and particularly in the latter case— there are two documents of vital importance which you should prepare. The first, to which I have already referred, is a note of the points which it is necessary to establish to set up your case or your defence; the second is a note of any salient points which you would wish to put in cross-examination to principal witnesses. I greatly deprecate the practice, even for the inexperienced, of writing out, as I know some advocates do, precisely the question which it is intended to ask the witness, each question being followed by the words, "If the answer is 'yes' ask . . . ; if 'no' ask . . . " Anyone who finds it necessary to perform this herculean task before daring to cross-examine is not cut out for advocacy and should forthwith turn to other fields to conquer.

There is necessarily a limit to the number of points which need to be put to particular witnesses which you can foresee in advance of the actual hearing. However, a note should be made to refresh your memory of inconsistencies made manifest by the disclosure of correspondence and documents generally; on differing versions contained within two or more previous statements of a witness or defendant and of other relevant and significant matters revealed by the pre-trial inquiries which you will have made. From then on you must necessarily improvise your questions as the evidence is revealed; it is, however, wise to decide in advance the line of questions with which you will commence the cross-examination of an important witness, and, where possible, the line of questions on which you will finish your cross-examination.

To this point we have been largely concerned with the technique of building up a case—but in framing your cross-examination there is one vitally important principle which must be followed: the need for elimination.

As we shall later consider, effective cross-examination is not only concerned with "what questions should I ask?" but no less important—and, perhaps, more important—"what questions can I omit?" Preliminary thought on these lines at the stage of preparation may well sow the seeds of later success.

Final preparation

You will then have reached the point at which you must make your final preparations for actually presenting the case to the court. You have satisfied yourself that you have subjected the case to the fullest possible investigation, the maximum of preparation. I cannot too often repeat that preparation in the presentation of cases to court is the real key to success. In the second place, you will have satisfied yourself that you have complete mastery of the facts and law which it will be your duty to present. Some of the finest advocates have been known to conduct long and complicated cases over many days without any further reference to their notes or to their papers. Few advocates can command ability of this order; if you are not one of that limited few you need not despair; but you should have a sufficient command of your case so that when you do, from time to time, glance at your notes or papers, you immediately recognise the points which you have noted, or the passages in the documents or proofs which you have marked as being of special significance. Most of the cases which will normally be conducted by newly qualified lawyers will be those which are relatively simple, and, in practice, the young advocate may find that he is required to appear in court, at short notice with insufficient time for adequate, or indeed, any preparation. On occasions, this may be unavoidable. However, principals, instructing solicitors and the courts must recognise that any case—be it large or small—requires proper preparation, and the interests of justice may well justify an adjournment for this purpose. To present a muddled or inadequate case for fear of offending those who require its immediate disposal is to forsake the interests of the client.

Cases of this sort apart, you will have retained with your papers, throughout the initial preparation, the statement of your objectives and the significant matters which you must prove. It is then desirable to prepare a chronological analysis of the times, dates and facts. I recommend that this be done on foolscap paper setting out the date in the first column, times in the second column, and a short, pithy, account of the facts in the third column. This, especially in a complicated case can be invaluable, since it enables you, as the witnesses give their evidence, immediately to fit any particular date or time to which they may refer into the chronological sequence in which the events happened. It also becomes a useful document when you come to address the court, particularly as an aide memoire, if for one moment or another your memory happens to fail you. Whilst in the early stages—and the later ones as well—you may be well advised to rely on notes, it is wise not to become their slave. The mind like any other part of the body tends to become less active the less it is used. The fact that the vast majority of speakers, judges, barristers and solicitors—even when speaking after dinner—must rely on notes is because they have habituated their minds to depend on them. Nothing can be substituted for the spontaneity and persuasiveness of those speakers who eschew them. When you can manage without them, try to do so.

You will have carefully marked and turned back the pages of the correspondence which is going to be produced to the court. In marking the correspondence you should select particular passages which may well form the basis for cross-examination, either because of the special significance of the particular document; because of manifest inaccuracies contained in one letter or another, or because, for some reason, the particular document is likely to be helpful to the proof of your case or to the destruction of the case of your opponent.

Prepare a note of your legal argument. This should follow the order in which you propose to present it to the court. I recommend that it be set down with brief statements of the law which you propose to expound and, inset and underneath each proposition, the full name and reference of the authority upon which you are going to rely. Setting down your argument in this fashion serves a twin purpose; not only does it enable you to have for ready reference the law, and the authority for the propositions which you are propounding, but it assists in clarifying your own mind as to the law applicable. A further important point is to ensure that you insert tabs, *i.e.* small pieces of paper, at the appropriate page of the law reports to which you are going to refer and have the reports and text books laid out in front of you in the order in which you intend to refer to them. There is nothing more destructive of a carefully prepared argument than repeated pauses and hesitancies whilst you feverishly search for the right page in order to read the report on which you seek to rely. If your case includes a claim for damages, prepare a careful summary of the heads under which they arise, and the arguments which support recoverability. Research similar cases to be used by way of comparison. If you are seeking orders from the court, draft that in advance and if this includes an injunction draft them as well. Finally, consider the position as to costs and the basis upon which you can seek orders for their recovery.

You will, I hope, also have prepared a list of the authorities so that you can hand this to the court usher well in advance of the commencement of your case, in order that he may be sure that the relevant reports are available for the court; moreover, if he requires it, supply a copy to your opponent. Your function is to assist justice—not to cheat by taking your opponent by surprise.

So much for the preparation. I have endeavoured to demonstrate that the technique of persuasion largely lies in the investigation and collation of evidence, without which all the histrionics and eloquence will count for little. That books on advocacy have hitherto dealt only with the latter and largely ignored the former is indicative, perhaps, of no more than that those who really win their clients' cases have been too busy searching for essential information to take time to describe for others how they do it.

II: The Ethics of Advocacy

Duties of an advocate

Whilst the primary function of an advocate is to present the case for his client to its best advantage, it is not his task to win the case as at all costs. When the duties of an advocate are examined it will become apparent that he is necessarily bound by certain ethical rules. Although these rules may in part have found their genesis in the need to preserve the integrity and dignity of the profession, it will almost invariably be found, on analysis, that they reflect the requirements of advocacy in its best and most effective form. They are matters of fundamental commonsense when applied against the principle that it is the function of the advocate to assist the court to reach a just decision on the facts properly adduced before it in accordance with a correct interpretation of the law. This duty may, on occasions, cause him to face perplexing questions as to how he can best reconcile his duty to the court with that which he owes to his client.

Good Faith

Certainly an advocate must never positively deceive the court; he must place before it all the information which the court is entitled to have; he must never state facts to the court which he believes to be untrue, and he must bring to the notice of the court every legal authority which his researches have revealed, even although they may be adverse to his client's case.

The primary duty of the advocate is to his client, although he has a concurrent duty to the court and the public. The duty to the client has its foundations, no doubt, in the law of agency. As between a solicitor-advocate and his client there is a legal contract of agency. Agency, however, does not require a contract for its creation; it is a relationship from which certain obligations flow. As a consequence the barrister, who does not enter into a contract with his client, merely regarding his fee as an honorarium for which he cannot sue, is equally the agent of the client, when appearing on his behalf.

The Basis of the Duty

The relationship of principal and agent is fiduciary, depending upon trust, which the courts will inexorably enforce. The agent, therefore, must never act against the principal's interest; he must make the fullest disclosure of any interest of a personal nature which he may have in his principal's affairs. As a corollary, he must never place himself in a situation where his interest conflicts with his duty. He must not make use, in any manner prejudicial to the principal, of any material or information acquired in the course of the agency, and, in addition to a duty to account, he owes, of course, a duty to take reasonable care in the performance of his principal's affairs.

A solicitor is an Officer of the Supreme Court, *i.e.* the High Court, the Court of Appeal and, since 1972, the Crown Court, and it is sometimes suggested that this is the basis of the extensive duty which he owes to the court. This, however, is not so, since he is not an officer of the county courts or the magistrates courts, but his duties to these courts are no different from those which he owes to the Supreme Court. Moreover, barristers are not officers of the court at all but their duties—as advocates—are the same as solicitors.

It would seem, therefore, that the only effect of solicitors being officers of the court is that it enables the court to discipline them, in some respects, in a more direct manner than it can others. The justification for this power which excludes the Bar may be thought to be, at least, questionable.

In this country we operate an adversary system of trial, the underlying philosophy of which is that each side is represented by an advocate whose task is to place his client's case before the court to its best advantage, consistent with fairness and integrity. It is then for the judge, in reliance on the observance of that principle, to decide the case on the material so placed before him.

The standard of skill, diligence and care which our adversary system requires of advocates is very high, and is considered by many to be immeasurably higher than in most other countries in the world. The judge, if justice is to be done, must feel assured that all relevant material and each sustainable argument has been advanced. Hence the imperative need for careful thought and attention to detail in the preparation of the case. By comparison, for example, in the United States, the judges sometimes employ clerks "to research" the law (and sometimes to marshal the arguments as well), when they feel unable to rely on some American advocates to place all relevant material and arguments before them.

Privilege

It is at this point that what, at first sight, appear to be dilemmas start to emerge. The efficient administration of justice requires that clients be free to reveal, however incriminating these may be, all material facts and information to their lawyers, whether solicitors or barristers, without fear that they may subsequently be disclosed to others. For this reason the law provides that any communication (except one aimed at constituting the lawyer the conscious or unconscious instrument in the furtherance of a fraud or crime) which is made by a person to a lawyer in his capacity as such is a privileged communication which the lawyer is under an obligation not to disclose. It requires little thought to appreciate how vital rules for the proper administration of Justice are, as they affect privilege.

Unless lawyers are given the whole of the facts it becomes impossible to advise or adequately conduct their cases. It is no less important that the advice which is given is also fully protected from disclosure. What prospect is there of such full disclosure being made to lawyers if it is possible for a court to compel disclosure? Citizens would be more than reluctant to disclose the truth if they knew that their lawyer could be compelled to reveal what he had been told thus placing them in the very danger which they had consulted lawyers to avoid. Moreover how could lawyers effectively assist the court if the clients were fearful of disclosing to them the totality of the facts?

For all these reasons, it has long been the law that the privilege from disclosure, and the right to waive it, rests exclusively with the client. It is his privilege alone and neither his lawyer nor anyone else can waive it, and until relatively recently it has been believed that the court lacked the ability to waive or over-ride it. Unhappily, there has been an increasing tendency in recent years to attack and to endeavour to diminish the protection from disclosure which privilege should provide. Increased and unwarranted powers have been afforded to the Inland Revenue, Customs and Excise and the Department of Trade, which, in practice, impinge so much on privilege as to have become wholly objectionable. Now, the courts themselves have shown an equal and, perhaps no less objectionable willingness to impair the protection which it afforded.

In 1972, at Lincoln Crown Court (*R.* v. *Barton* [1973] 1 W.L.R. 115) an application was made to the trial judge, Caulfield, J., for leave to cross-examine a solicitor to the personal representatives of an estate on certain documents, which it was agreed, were otherwise privileged; They were not the subject of any charge against the defendant, or such as would be produced in evidence by the prosecution. Moreover, the trial judge was not even apprised of the relevance of the information which the documents might contain, other than that counsel for the accused assured him that justice would not be done unless the disclosure was possible. On the advice of the Law Society, the solicitor claimed privilege on behalf of the clients' Personal Representatives. The judge explained that since they were on circuit, facilities for research were difficult; he appears to have had only one case, which evidently, so far as the report shows, was not on the actual point, and *Cross on Evidence*, on which to rely. In fact, even with proper research it would have been found that no previous authority existed, in any event. Applying what he conceived to be the rules of natural justice, he purported to waive the privilege on the principle that this was permissible "to establish innocence or refute an allegation made by the Crown." Hardly, it may be thought a satisfactory basis for overruling a principle which had endured for very many years, and without any argument as to the vital consequences which might result from such a change in the law.

The question was next considered by the Court of Appeal (*R.* v. *Ataou* [1988] 1 Q.B. 799). The appellant had, during the trial, sought to elicit from his solicitor, who had previously also acted for his co-accused who had been acquitted, a statement alleged to have been made by the co-accused, when the solicitor was advising him, which went towards exculpating the appellant. The trial judge had held that the statement was privileged (as manifestly it was) and had refused to allow the solicitor to be cross-examined as to the contents despite the fact that the co-accused had given evidence to the contrary. Some may consider that the judge with commendable instinct (since the matter does not seem to have been fully argued) must have had regard to the wider and general requirements of justice, rather than to the particular.

The Court of Appeal, so far as the report indicates, did not hear arguments as to such wider issues as they arose in depth, and neither the Law Society nor the Bar Council were invited to address the court *amicus curiae*. The court, whilst noting that the Solicitor was in breach of his duty of confidentiality to their former client in disclosing the previous statement of the co-accused to the Appellant's advisers, held that in such circumstances "it should be for the defendant to show, on the balance of probabilities that the claim (to privilege) cannot be sustained. That might be done by demonstrating that there is no ground on which the client could any longer reasonably be regarded as having a recognisable interest in asserting the privilege. The judge must then balance whether the legitimate interest of the defendant in seeking to breach the privilege outweighs that of the client in seeking to maintain it."

Finally, the matter fell to be considered in the Guinness trial (*R.* v. *Saunders and others*) which is thus far unreported. Henry J. decided that he was bound by the decision of the Court of Appeal. He referred to the case of *Marks* v. *Bathus* (1890) Q.B.D. 494, and to cases concerning Crown privilege for the proposition that information must not be withheld as a matter of public policy, which tends to establish innocence, as well as several Commonwealth cases. He indicated that the need for the judge to engage in the balancing exercise described in *Ataou* did not arise if the need to maintain the privilege could not be established. Holding that it had been established in the instant case, he decided further that the interest of the defence in having it waived outweighed the interest of the clients in maintaining the privilege. He observed that whilst this rule obtained in relation to the establishing of innocence it could not be invoked to adduce evidence tending to establish guilt.

Whilst these cases clearly raise a most important and difficult problem vital to the administration of justice, it is regrettable that this new principle is emerging without the far wider implications being argued and considered at length. Clearly, it calls for a decision of the House of Lords.

What are some of the considerations which arise? First, from its very nature, and the circumstances which give rise to it, there are always matters withheld from the court, by reason of privilege, which, if revealed. might better assist a court to reach a just decision. The only justification for withholding it is that to permit otherwise could so undermine the client and lawyer relationship that clients would be unlikely to unburden themselves fully to their adviser. Currently, they have done so on the assurance of their lawyers that whatever they may tell them is totally privileged from disclosure, unless they otherwise agree. Must lawyers now tell their clients instead that this is the position unless a judge later decides otherwise? And if the lawyer fails to alert his client to this risk is he negligent? It would seem that he would be.

As the quoted authorities show, the court should not waive the privilege to assist a defendant if it involves disclosure of privileged material which tends to point to the guilt of the client who seeks to maintain the privilege. In those circumstances, presumably, the interests of justice, as they affect the particular accused takes second place. If so, why should it be otherwise, where it is clearly essential to preserve the sacrosanct nature of privileged communications? Should not the wider interests of so many take precedence over the particular interest of one individual?

Perhaps the whole subject of privilege and disclosure needs urgent review, especially since there are many other aspects which call for clarification. For example, in discovery in civil proceedings, all relevant documents must be disclosed to the opposing side, other than documents prepared for the purpose of litigation. How is this to be reconciled with the more general proposition that all material imparted to a lawyer in relation to his clients affairs is already protected by the existing rules?

However, much as problems of this intensity may worry advocates, no one can deny their fascination.

Concurrent Duties

How then does an advocate reconcile his duty not to deceive the court, with his obligation to his client to keep secret all information imparted to him? If a lawyer is instructed to defend an accused person, who tells him he is guilty, how can he plead "not guilty" on his behalf and defend him? Does he not deceive the court by pretending that his client is innocent when he knows he is guilty? This problem, in its most extreme form, provides a perennial question for discussion whenever a lull develops in conversation between a guest and a lawyer at a cocktail party.

In the first place, a plea of "not guilty" is not synonymous with declaring "I am innocent." Our criminal process is accusatorial; the onus rests upon the prosecution to prove the accused guilty on the evidence, beyond reasonable doubt. The plea of "not guilty" is no more than a procedural formula by which the accused puts the prosecution to proof of its case. It is no more a deception than the comparable situation on the pleadings in a civil suit, when the defendant denies the truth of an assertion in the plaintiff's statement of claim, in order to put him to proof of it.

The proper course for the advocate to pursue, therefore, in those circumstances, is to put the prosecution to proof of its case, to which end, he may, and indeed should, cross-examine the prosecution witnesses in order to demonstrate their unreliability or incredibility; he may take objection to the competency of the court or the form of the indictment or charge and should raise objection to, and argue against, the admissibility of any evidence which appears to be improperly adduced. He should submit (or if, when a solicitor has instructed counsel to conduct a case) cause to be submitted, where appropriate, that there is insufficient evidence to justify a conviction or should advance any other defence open to the client, short of a protestation of innocence. It would, however, be wholly improper to suggest that some other person had committed the offence charged.

If, however, the client insists upon giving evidence in the witness box or making a statement indicating innocence, or requires the case to be conducted in such a fashion as asserts his innocence, e.g. by calling evidence in support of a false alibi, the advocate must decline to act. To do otherwise would be to take part in an attempt to deceive the court. In withdrawing from the case, the advocate should not merely absent himself from the hearing but should, out of courtesy to the court, attend, at his own expense, to indicate that he finds himself unable to continue to represent the accused. He should give no reason, since the reason is the subject of privilege. Having withdrawn from the case he should, if a solicitor, take steps to remove his name, or that of his firm, from the record. If asked—and far more—if pressed by the court (however unlikely this may be) to explain his withdrawal, he should merely reply that the question is one which he should not be asked, and which, in any event, he is unable to answer by reason of professional privilege.

The Guilty Client

It is sometimes said that an advocate who is told by his client that he his guilty, should suggest to, or advise, the client that it would be better for him to seek other representation, because the new advocate would not be embarrassed by the knowledge of his guilt. The propriety of this is questionable, in so much as it might amount to encouragement by the first advocate to the client to deceive the court by giving evidence as to his innocence, with the aid of a second advocate who commits no breach of professional duty because he is not informed as to his guilt. In such circumstances the right course for the advocate to adopt is to indicate to his client the limitations which the admission places on his conduct of the defence. These are, as already mentioned, that he can require the prosecution fully to prove their case in accordance with the evidence, that he may take technical objections and may argue that there is insufficient evidence to justify a conviction, but he cannot put forward any arguments suggesting that some other person has committed the offence charged or otherwise protesting his client's innocence. If the consequence of this advice is that the client decides to seek the services of another advocate that is his affair.

Judgment as to Guilt

What, however, if the client does not admit guilt, but, in the light of his experience and judgment, the advocate forms his own view that he is guilty? Does he then deceive the court by continuing to act? If an advocate refused, or was precluded by professional rules from undertaking, to represent an accused because he believed him to be guilty, he would be interposing his judgment between the citizen and the court, which he has no right to do. The decision as to whether the accused is guilty is one for a competent court. It is not a matter for decision by the advocate and questions directed to eliciting a private admission by the client are neither relevant nor valuable and can be very embarrassing. Anything short of a clear admission of guilt in no way trammels the conduct of the advocate. Every citizen accused of crime is entitled to be tried, with adequate representation, by a court having jurisdiction to try him. Experience, in any case, shows that a jury will often take a different view from that of the advocate, and even he, when he has seen the prosecution witnesses give their evidence may alter his own opinion.

The situation has never, perhaps, been better put than by Erskine in defence of Tom Paine (State Trials XXXII.411) when he said:

> "From the moment that any advocate can be permitted to say that he will or will not stand between the crown and the subject arraigned in the court where he sits daily to practise, from that moment the liberties of England are at an end. If the advocate refuses to defend from what he may think of the charge or the defence, he assumes the character of the judge; nay, he assumes it before the hour of judgment, and in proportion to his rank and reputation puts the heavy influence of perhaps a mistaken opinion into the scale against the accused, in whose favour the benevolent principle of the English law makes all presumptions and which commands the very judge to be his counsel."

This is a passage which all advocates should read and read again, and which those few police officers who consider that their personal judgment as to the guilt of the accused should be decisive, could read with no less justification, mark, lean and inwardly digest, in relation to their comparable, although necessarily different duty.

This seeming dilemma frequently arises in motoring cases where the advocate is told by the client of previous motoring convictions of which the court and prosecution are unaware. What the advocate must not do is to conduct the case, or address the court, upon the basis of positive assertions that his client has an unblemished record. For example, in addressing the court in mitigation of penalty, it would be wholly improper, in those circumstances, for the advocate to say to the court, "as you have seen, my client has an unblemished record, having driven motor vehicles for thirty years without a single conviction." His proper course is wholly to eschew any reference to his client's character as a driver, or indeed otherwise, and to limit his mitigation only to the circumstances in which this particular accident or offence occurred. This may, at first sight, appear to be a piece of legal sophistry. If, however, it is considered in the context of the imperative need to preserve the client's privilege, for the reasons already explained, whilst at the same time requiring an advocate, against that duty to the client, not to violate his duty to the court, it will be seen that no other course could be devised which is reconcilable between these two conflicting principles.

The problem can become still more intense when the facts known to the advocate, but unknown to the court, go wholly or partly to the jurisdiction of the court. Take for example the case where a defendant is charged with an offence and the advocate knows that this, being his third conviction for a totting-up offence, the court has an obligation to disqualify him unless in all the circumstances it may otherwise order. The dilemma facing the advocate is that if he addresses the court in mitigation he ought properly to have in mind the possibility of the court imposing disqualification; if he does not address the court, the penalty which the court imposed might be disproportionate to the offence charged. If, however, he does address the court, and is to deal with the question of disqualification he cannot do so without referring to his client's record and making a full disclosure. The prudent course in those circumstances is to advise the client to allow him to make the disclosure; if the client refuses to do so, he might well deem it advisable to withdraw from the case. If however the client insists on his conducting it, the most he can do is to avoid any reference to disqualification or character in mitigation whatsoever. It is unlikely that these particular circumstances would normally arise, since the convictions are usually recorded on the driving licence, which has to be produced before the final disposal of the case. Exceptionally, however, it can occur, especially where an accused person has in the meanwhile obtained, by one means or another, a new licence, on which previous convictions are not recorded. However, as will later be seen, there may well be circumstances in which, as part of the technique of persuasion, it would be wise to disclose antecedents or character, which are unknown to the court, with a view to obtaining a better result for the client than might otherwise be the case.

Conflicting Statements

A difficult question frequently arises where facts are disclosed by the client to the advocate which might, on an objective assessment, lead to an irresistible inference of guilt by the advocate if he exercised a personal judgment.

Suppose the client makes a series of statements to the advocate, before or during the proceedings, which are inconsistent with one another. Should the advocate, in those circumstances, refuse to act further on the client's behalf? It does not inevitably follow that he should, since, as has already been seen, it is not the advocate's function to judge his own client. This is the function of the court. The advocate should, however, closely question the client as to the content and basis of the later statements. If, for example, the client says that he has altered his original statement as he thought it unlikely to be accepted by the court, this means that he proposes to perjure himself at the trial and, unless he accepts the advocate's advice to restrict his evidence to the truth, the advocate should decline to act any further. If, however, an explanation is advanced which might be bona fide, even though the advocate himself entertains doubts about it, it is not for the advocate but for the court to assess the accuracy of the matter, and the advocate is both justified and indeed under a duty to continue to act. In this connection the position of the advocate is exactly the same if he is preparing the case as a solicitor or enquiring into it as a barrister prior to actually assuming the function of the advocate. If, however, the advocate adduces evidence to the court, through or on the instructions of the client, which the client later admits to be perjury, it is the advocate's duty to decline to act further in the proceedings unless the client, having been so advised, is willing to disclose his conduct fully to the court. As a moment's reflection shows, were it otherwise this would not only involve participation by the advocate in a deliberate deception of the court but it would also make the advocate, in the absence of full disclosure, the client's agent in the commission of the criminal offence of perjury.

If the court puts any questions to a defendant as to his character, where it is not in issue, or if the court should address a question to the advocate as to the character of the defendant, the proper reply for the advocate is that the question is not one which should be put to the defendant; nor is it a question for him personally to answer and he should refuse to allow the defendant to reply, or for that matter to vouchsafe any information himself.

Duty to Require Proof

One of the functions which an advocate must perform is to discuss with his client and to advise him whether or not he should give evidence in his own defence. The decision, however, should always rest with the accused. If he instructs his advocate that he is not guilty of the offence, but is unwilling to give evidence, it is nevertheless the duty of the advocate to ensure that his defence is put before the court; if necessary the advocate should make suggestions of a positive nature to the witnesses as to his client's innocence and he could indeed call witnesses on his client's behalf. It is necessary to stress that we are here discussing a case where the client is declaring his innocence; as we have seen, the situation is wholly different where the client has admitted his guilt to the advocate.

There is one aspect of this particular problem which has never, it is suggested, been properly examined or defined. Where a solicitor is himself preparing the case and presenting it to the court the rules which are described above clearly have full application. It frequently occurs, however, that a case is prepared by a solicitor who then instructs a barrister to present the case to the court. What then is the position of the barrister and solicitor if the solicitor has been told by the client that he is guilty? Must he disclose this fact to the barrister? Or should he, in the client's interests, withhold it from the barrister, in order that he should not personally be embarrassed in presenting the matter to the court? It is perhaps surprising that there appears to be no decision upon this matter to be called in aid for guidance. One suspects, as a matter of practice, that some solicitors would not in those circumstances tell the barrister and that the barrister in those same circumstances would not wish to be told. However, it is suggested that this is hardly a practice which could be justified on ethical principles; indeed, it could not bring credit to the legal profession, if attempts were made to justify conduct of this sort. If it be right, as it surely must be, that both the barrister and the solicitor are agents of the principal, and that the knowledge of the principal and the agent is the knowledge of the other then, putting the matter at its lowest, the solicitor would be deliberately withholding information from his brother agent, the barrister, in order that the barrister could then innocently mislead the court. If it is not the rule, then it should be the rule, that the knowledge of matters which require a critical judgment to be formed in order to avoid misleading the court must be imparted by the representative of each branch of the legal profession to the other in relation to the conduct of any given case. The proper course, it is suggested, where these circumstances arise, is for the solicitor to disclose the true facts to the barrister and for both to withdraw from the case.

Technical Defences

From time to time lawyers are subjected to criticism for raising technical defences on behalf of clients in criminal trials when the case is in truth devoid of merit. This criticism, probably reached its high water mark in relation to charges under the Road Safety Acts in regard to drink and driving.

A court of law is not concerned to make moral judgments but to ascertain the facts and apply the law in relation to them. The law, and the criminal law in particular, is a series of rules laid down either at Common Law, or by Parliament in statutes, under which citizens forego some of their rights to protect the rights and freedoms of the remainder. Were the courts or the lawyers to construe statutes according to what each court or lawyer believed to be the justice of the case the rights of the majority of the public would become increasingly diluted. Thus it may, with truth, be said that the importance of ensuring that the person is not convicted of an offence which has not been clearly defined by Parliament finds its justification in ensuring that the courts do not take unto themselves powers in excess of those defined by the Common Law or by Parliament. It thus follows that an advocate has the same right as the client to assert and to defend his client's rights and to protect his liberty; indeed it is his duty. He must state every fact freely and use every argument, whether technical or otherwise, which can, in accordance with the law and within rules of professional conduct properly be made. Far from failing in his duty to the public, he is fulfilling a duty towards it, when he raises a technical defence on the wording of a statute, even although had the statute been worded differently the clear absence of merits in the case would have justified a conviction. Thus if Parliament states, as it did under the Road Safety Act that to be guilty of an offence under the Act the accused must have been driving with a greater amount of alcohol in his blood than the limits permitted by the Act, it is wholly proper for a lawyer to argue that such a period of time had elapsed before the accused was required to subject himself to a breathalyser test that he was no longer driving within the meaning of that phrase in the Act. Indeed, if such a defence is available to the client, the advocate is not only performing his duty in advancing it but may be negligent if he fails to do so.

Inventing Defence

However, this does not mean that an advocate must ever, in relation to the facts, invent a defence for his client. A defendant often says to an advocate, "If you believe that my story is unlikely to be accepted, what do you suggest that I should say?" Under no circumstances must an advocate ever suggest to a clients words which he should use, evidence which he should give, or a defence, by distortion of the facts, which he should raise. To do so is clearly highly improper conduct which no reputable advocate should ever countenance for one moment.

Disclosing all Legal Authorities

The situation in relation to the law is wholly different from that applicable to the facts. The law is part of the public fund of knowledge. If an advocate discovers or knows of a decision which is adverse to his case, he must not conveniently forget its existence for fear of damaging his client's case. His bounden duty to the court is then to draw the authority to the attention of the court and to seek, where possible, to distinguish the facts in the instant case from those of the reported authority or endeavour to show that the authority was wrongly decided, or that, despite the adverse decision, the matter can otherwise be resolved in his client's favour. Moreover, in advance of the actual hearing, wherever possible, the advocate should draw his opponent's attention to any authority which he has discovered, including any which is against his contention, in order that the court may have the benefit of adequate argument on the authority after mature consideration. This is a rule of general application, it obtains whenever an advocate appears and whatever the type of tribunal before which the case is being conducted.

Disclosure of Facts

The facts which are disclosed to the advocate by the client are not public property as is the case with the law. They are protected by the privilege of the client which, subject to what is described earlier, he alone can waive. The advocate, therefore, except where it amounts to a positive misleading of the court, is under no duty to bring facts to the notice of the court which may be damaging to his client's case, indeed, by reason of the client's privilege he is precluded from doing so. Similarly, he is under no duty to undo the consequences of the court being misled on the facts by the prosecution. If, however, the failure to disclose facts known to the advocate would, in the context of the words used by the advocate when addressing the court, or from the words used by the witnesses called by him, amount to a positive deception of the court, *e.g.* if he is instructed by the client to assert his innocence when he has been told by the client that he is guilty, the only course open to the advocate is to withdraw from the case.

Similarly, for example, where the character of a police officer is relevant in a civil case and it is known to the advocate, but not to the court, that between the institution of the proceedings and the hearing, the officer had been subject to disciplinary proceedings and demoted from inspector to sergeant, the advocate must not continue to refer to the witness as "Mr," by which prefix inspectors are frequently addressed, nor instruct the witness not to wear uniform (from which his reduced rank would be evident) when appearing in court. This is a course of conduct calculated to deceive the court and is to be distinguished from presenting the case without directly informing the court of the disciplinary proceedings (of which he had learned under the cloak of privileges).

What is the situation if, after the conclusion of the evidence and argument, but before judgment is given, an advocate discovers a proposition of law which is relevant? He should, with his opponent's concurrence, submit it to the judge. If, however, after discussing the matter with his opponent, the advocate who discovered the authority continues to believe it is relevant but his opponent disagrees, the proper course is for the first advocate to submit the additional authority to the judge and to inform his opponent that he has done so. (If this is done in open court it will obviously be done orally; if judgment has been reserved, the opponent should be sent a copy of the letter to the judge.) In any event, the judge should be told that the opponent has been consulted and either agrees or disagrees that the authority is relevant.

Although the rules laid down for the guidance of the Bar would appear to indicate the contrary, it is considered that where a judge is in danger of misleading himself on the law, without having called upon the advocates to deal with the particular point on which he is pronouncing, the advocate should nevertheless draw the judge's attention to any authority known to the advocate which the judge appears to have overlooked.* The advocate must not, however, put before the court arguments which he knows to be unsound. Apart from being tactically unwise it is unethical: as Lord Denning M.R.

* Boulton, *Conduct and Etiquette at the Bar*, Fifth Edition p. 75; Statement of Bar Council, 1971–72, p. 34.

said** of one advocate "appearing . . . on behalf of an accused person, it was as I understand it, his duty to take any point which he believed to be fairly arguable on behalf of his client. An advocate is not to usurp the province of the judge. He is not to determine what shall be the effect of legal argument. He is not guilty of misconduct simply because he takes a point which the tribunal holds to be bad. He only becomes guilty of misconduct if he is dishonest. That is, if he knowingly takes a bad point and thereby deceives the court."

Assisting the Court

If in a criminal case some irregularity comes to the advocate's knowledge before the decision of the court is given, he should bring it to the attention of the court, and not hold it in reserve for appeal, when it may be too late to remedy the mistake. Similarly, if a procedural defect exists, *e.g.* an error in the chain of events due to a typographical mistake, which might invalidate the proceedings, he should not defer drawing it to the attention of the court, especially by waiting until it is too late to remedy it. In many cases, failure to do so will merely involve amendment and delay. The successful outcome of a case must never be achieved by the chicanery of the advocate on whose integrity and assistance the court must at all times feel able to depend.

Insulting Questions

From time to time clients will try to persuade an advocate to put questions to witnesses which are intended only to insult, degrade, or annoy either the opponent, the witness, or some other person. Not only is it contrary to an advocate's duty to do so, but it would be improper conduct for him to submit to such pressure.

He should, moreover, never put questions as to character or credibility unless he believes them to be well founded or true. An advocate in a court, particularly one which is conducted in public, is in a unique position to damage the reputation of those who perhaps cannot answer for themselves and it is right that he should

---

** *Abraham* v. *Jutsun* (1963) 2 All E.R. 402, at p. 404.

carefully ensure that nothing which he does is directed to causing difficulties for others or damage to their reputation. The power which he has in this regard is one which he must exercise with a due sense of responsibility. It is his function to exercise his own judgment both as to the substance and the form of the questions which he will put to the witnesses. He should never allow his personal feelings to intrude and he should at all times act with due courtesy towards the court, his opponents and all other persons concerned in the case.

In order to put matters in cross-examination, it is not essential that the advocate should be able to prove by affirmative evidence the allegations which he is putting. If it is necessary to put questions involving allegations of fraud, misconduct or the commission of any criminal offence, he must satisfy himself that no reason exists for believing that they are intended only to attack the character of the witness, and that there is good reason to believe they are well founded or true. Courtesy should be the handmaiden of good advocacy.

Advocate as Witness

It is clearly undesirable that an advocate should place himself into a situation in which he is liable to appear both as an advocate and as a witness. If it becomes obvious that he may have to give evidence on behalf of the client he should withdraw from the case, unless his evidence is a matter of the merest formality. An advocate who withdraws from the conduct of a case must take steps to ensure that an accused person is never left unrepresented. If this situation arises before the commencement of the hearing he should inform the client of his intention to withdraw from the case in sufficient time to enable him to obtain alternative representation, or an adjournment of the hearing. If this proves impossible or if the necessity to withdraw from the case arises after the trial has commenced the advocate should give all possible assistance to the client and the court to facilitate suitable alternative arrangements.

Needless to say adequate grounds must exist for determining a retainer. This is a question of law and not merely of ethics. The absence of such grounds or the failure to ensure that the client has sufficient notice or assistance in making alternative arrangements might well give rise to an action for breach of contract or negligence in the case of a solicitor and to disciplinary proceedings in respect of both barristers and solicitors.

The Prosecuting Advocate

In contrast, a prosecuting advocate in a criminal trial assumes something of the character of a Minister of Justice. The prosecuting advocate, to quote the words of Hilbery J.*: "must see to it that every material point is made which supports the prosecution case or destroys the case put forward for the defence. But as prosecuting counsel he should not regard his task as one of winning the case. He is an officer of justice. He must present the case against the prisoner relentlessly but with scrupulous fairness. He is not to make merely forensic points or debating scores." He must not conceal from his opponent facts which are within his knowledge although inconsistent with the case presented to the court. He should disclose to his opponent any criminal convictions known to him which have been recorded in respect of any of the witnesses upon whom he intends to rely; if he knows of witnesses who may be able to give evidence to assist the defence, and whom he does not intend to call as witnesses, he should, at least, provide his opponent with their names and addresses, and, in his discretion, may be willing to provide copies of statements. If, in the course of the trial, one of his witnesses gives evidence on a material matter which differs from the facts disclosed by the witness in the proof of evidence in the advocate's possession, it is his duty to show the statement to his opponent so that the opponent may be able to cross-examine the witness as to the fact that the evidence which he is giving is inconsistent with the statements which he had earlier made. These duties which are cast upon the prosecuting advocate are consistent with the requirements of British justice that no unfair advantage should at any time be taken against a citizen whose reputation and liberty are at stake in criminal proceedings. In similar vein, the prosecutor should always present his case dispassionately; he should not attempt by advocacy to induce the court to

* See *Duty and Art in Advocacy* (1959), p. 10.

impose a more severe sentence. Some advocates (fortunately rare) open the case for the prosecution in emotive and tendentious terms. Thus it is not for the advocate to express his own opinion to the court when describing the condition of a machine alleged to have resulted in the death of a third party as "a death trap"; the position would be quite different if an expert witness whom he was proposing to call had so described the machine, in which case it would be proper to point out to the court that the evidence will involve the allegation that the machine constituted "a death trap." Nor is a prosecuting advocate justified in including in his opening his own opinions as to the wickedness of character, either directly or by implication, of the accused. I recall an occasion in my early days, when my enthusiasm sometimes outstripped my judgment. I was prosecuting in respect of a serious assault. The accused, who had allegedly attacked his girl friend, was by occupation a professional wrestler, appearing under the name of "Gentleman Jim," which was his professional, but not his true name. I opened the case to the magistrate in the following way: "In this case the Defendant is a professional wrestler known as "Gentleman Jim," but according to my instructions, his name is not Jim and he is no gentleman." I am not today as proud of that opening, which attracted attention in the local press, as I imagine I must have been then. No advocate should ever use his position to poke fun in any way at an accused person.

The prosecuting advocate must never deliberately withhold anything which is likely to assist the accused, and, in any case, it is not good advocacy, even tactically, to do so. This is another lesson which could more frequently be taken to heart by police officers when they give evidence in court. The prosecutor, who gives the impression of an overweening anxiety to secure a conviction; who feels the need to interrupt or nullify every point made for the defence, however small, or to cross-examine in an aggressive fashion, is far more likely to arouse the displeasure of the court, or even, psychologically, to enlist its sympathy in favour of the defence. A prosecutor or a prosecution witness who presents the facts in a reasoned and measured way, giving the clear impression that his only part in the proceedings is, as it should be, to ensure that the relevant material is fairly put before the court is far more likely to secure a conviction where justice requires it than by behaving in an unpleasant and aggressive way.

It is the duty of the prosecuting advocate—or, where two or more are engaged, one of them, to be present throughout the trial, including, in the higher courts, the summing-up, and the return of the jury; failure to attend in this way would mean that the advocate could not fully assist the court, as it is his duty to do. Moreover, he should, at the conclusion of the summing-up, draw the court's attention to any apparent errors or omissions of facts or law which are material and which seem to require correction. No such duty rests on the defending advocate though he may so address the court if he deems it necessary in the interest of his client.

Discovery

The question is frequently asked, particularly by police officers, why the defending advocate is not under a corresponding duty to that of the prosecuting advocate to reveal all the facts which come to his knowledge and to present the matter with that degree of objectivity and impartiality which is required of a prosecutor. There are indeed some who go further and suggest that the criminal process should be altered, to bring it more into conformity with the civil procedure, so that there is mutual discovery of documents and of certain of the essential facts and issues. This is no place to debate the merits—or in the writer's view, the demerits—of this contention. The reason for the present rule, however, needs to be clearly borne in mind. The fundamental principle on which the English criminal process rests is that the onus of proof lies, in general, on the prosecution throughout the case. Any change which would involve disclosure by the defence of material in their possession which was possibly harmful to their own case, would necessarily dilute the basic principle as to the onus of proof. It is this reason and this reason alone which justifies the present rule which draws a clear distinction between the respective functions of an advocate when prosecuting and defending.

Control of the Case

The solicitor advocate is in a contractual position in relation to his client. He in fact enters into a contract with the client to represent him and it is sometimes said that, as a consequence, he can only do those things in the conduct of a case which the client instructs him to do. On the other hand, it is also said that a barrister is "in control of the case" and has virtually a free hand to conduct the advocacy as he deems proper.* Whilst, however, the law remains as settled by the House of Lords in the case of *Rondel* v. *Worsley*** there is no difference between the position of a solicitor advocate and a barrister advocate when conducting proceedings in court. It seems probable, therefore, that the true position may more correctly be stated as follows: whereas barristers and solicitors are agents of the client, as mentioned earlier, the nature of their engagement is such that they cannot reasonably be expected constantly to stop the course of proceedings in order to take instructions on every aspect of the conduct of the case. It probably arises by implication, into the solicitor's contract of retainer and the terms of the barristers agency that, in pursuit of the advocacy, each of them is free to conduct the proceedings in such way as he, in his proper discretion, considers appropriate; if, however, on any particular matter the client has given express instructions to the advocate not to pursue a particular course, then, whether he be barrister or solicitor, he cannot override those instructions. If he is justifiably unwilling or unable to comply with them, it is his duty to advise the client that he cannot accept the instructions and that he must determine his retainer and withdraw from the case.

Such then are the fundamentals of the ethics of advocacy. There will certainly be occasions when the proper course to be pursued will be difficult to determine, but, as in so many pursuits, the path of honesty is invariably safest and, additionally, as the old adage affirms, the best policy. In the end, however, a court which is confident that the advocate appearing before it is competent and anxious to assist in reaching the proper decision is, from this fact alone, if the underlying arguments are sound, two-thirds of the way towards being persuaded to the acceptance of the client's case.

* See Boulton, *Conduct and Etiquette at the Bar*, p. 78; and *Cordery on Solicitors*, Chap. 6, pp. 103–105.
** [1967] 3 All E.R. 933.

III: The Strategy and Tactics of Advocacy

"The Appreciation of the Situation"

The conduct of a trial at law is, in many respects, comparable with the conduct of a military operation. Going to law is a great deal like going to war. Too many of those coming fresh to the practice of advocacy—and, regrettably, some of those whom experience should have taught better—pursue their task with inadequate pre-thought and often without any hint of analysis as to the needs of the objectives involved.

It is true that the novice is unlikely to be called upon to conduct a case of such weight as might be compared with a full scale war or even a major battle, but the strategy and tactics involved in a minor skirmish differ little, if at all, from that involved in a major undertaking.

Whether the case is large or small it is, of course, vital to have mastered the facts and the law applicable; essential to have researched every aspect of each so that there is full confidence in one's ability to face the court or tribunal. This, however, is not enough. Cases are not won by "playing it by ear" in the hope, if not the belief, that "it will be alright on the day." Yet, far too many advocates perform in this manner, believing it adequate to have read the papers, and some, it is often too obvious, not having even progressed that far.

It has been earlier noted that the first and vital essential in persuasion is to determine your objectives; to ask oneself "What am I seeking to achieve by this exercise." Yet, how many advocates, having mastered the facts and law and before entering Court, have sat down and asked themselves what is to be the plan of campaign? Fewer, I suspect, than should. Learn then from the Generals; they learned the dangers of neglecting this practice way back in the mists of time.

The first essential task placed upon a military commander in regard to strategy and tactics is to prepare "an appreciation of the situation." This is a review of the military problem or situation based on all available information, culminating in a plan of the action to be taken to meet the situation which has or may have to be faced. For preference it is committed to paper, and should follow the obvious logical sequence: (i) The object to be attained; (ii) the factors which effect the attainment of the object; (iii) courses of action open to the commander and the enemy; and finally (iv) the plan. A competent advocate should conduct his preparation for trial in a fashion not one whit different.

The Plan

Just as in war the same analysis must be made in the parts of a battle as distinct from the totality of the operation, in advocacy the same three considerations should be applied to the manner of dealing with individual witnesses and different aspects of the case in hand. In each case it should result in a plan, and, as General Wavell has observed, "the plan should be simple, as are almost all good plans in war." Moreover, in formulating it, another military maxim may equally be called in aid to "concentrate all available force at the decisive point."

If one studies the work of the great advocates the following of a preconceived plan can frequently be perceived. It is a most fruitful and fascinating exercise to sit through the hearing of cases and observe the experts or, as already recommended, to study the cases recorded in the series of Notable British Trials, and to identify the overall strategy which the advocates employed and the planned progress of their cross-examination of witnesses. It may seem when listened to in Court, or when read in those volumes, a spontaneous brilliant sortie; in every instance, deep and careful thought has preceded the master's undertaking.

Let us examine one famous example: in 1931 Alfred Arthur Rouse was tried for Murder and the Prosecution was conducted by the great Norman Birkett K.C., M.P. It was alleged that Rouse had deliberately set fire to his car, having rendered unconscious an unidentified man to whom he had given a lift, and had left him in the car to burn to death. An important, although by no means decisive aspect of the case, was the manner in which the fire had occurred, since Rouse asserted that the fire had accidentally begun. The engine of the car had a petrol union joint, of which both the male and female parts were constructed of brass. The Crown suggested that Rouse had loosened the nut before lighting the fire, in order to increase the flow of petrol and adduced expert evidence in support of this theory. Two days before the trial ended a businessman, who described himself as an engineer and fire assessor, contacted the defence and volunteered to give evidence, as he did on the last day of the trial. He said that the intense heat generated when petrol driven vehicles caught fire invariably loosened such nuts and that it was not, therefore, safe to infer that Rouse had loosened the nut on this joint.

Norman Birkett, in what became a much discussed cross-examination, began by asking the witness "What is the co-efficient of the expansion of brass?"

"I am afraid I cannot answer that question off-hand," was the reply.

"If you do not know, say so. What do I mean by the term?"

'You want to know what is the expansion of the metal under heat."

"I asked you what is the co-efficient of the expansion of brass." "Do you know what it means?", persisted Birkett.

"Put that way," replied the witness, "probably I do not."

"You are an engineer?"

"I dare say I am. I am not a doctor, nor a crime investigator, nor an amateur detective. I am an engineer."

"What is the co-efficient of the expansion of brass?" Birkett again asked. "You do not know?"

"No, not put that way" the witness rather lamely replied.

Clearly, it may be said, the tactics were designed to discredit the witness, and this had no less clearly been achieved. More, however, had been planned than that. In the subsequent discussion of this case it has been suggested that Birkett's question was a trick question and unworthy of him. He had gambled, it was suggested, and would have been discomfited if, as was possible, the witness had come up with the correct answer. Such criticism ignored the care and thought which doubtless preceded the framing of questions by one of the greatest advocates of recent generations. In general, different metals expand under heat and later contract to a constant extent. Since both the nut and the joint were made of brass, Birkett, given the right co-efficient in answer would merely have suggested, as he did in later questions, that one part would not have been any more loose against the other than it would have been before the fire began.

Moreover, whilst it might be said, as indeed it was, by the witness that the method of casting or rolling might have caused a different result if the nut and the joint were made from brass of different sources of manufacture, Birkett must also have realised that the witness, having only recently volunteered his evidence, could have had no time in which to ascertain, even if it were possible, the origins of the nut and joint to which he had not had access.

Such are the plans which emerge from a proper "appreciation of the situation." So much for a cause célèbre which is unlikely to fall into the lap of a mere tyro. The technique, however, is no different with far less important and routine cases.

The Analysis

Assume you have been consulted by a lady from Nigeria who has been charged with shop-lifting. She vigorously denies the charge. She tells you she had gone to a large chemists store to purchase presents for her return home after a visit to Britain for ten days. She had frequently shopped in the same store, and that very morning having arrived there at 11.30 a.m. spent £120.00 for which she had produced to you the receipts. She is the wife of a most important government official and her plane is scheduled to leave at 2 p.m. that afternoon.

She was in a great hurry; she had to visit a sick relative, make other purchases elsewhere; change a considerable quantity of American dollars into sterling, collect her luggage and get to the Airport by 1 p.m.

The store was very busy, and having gone to the first floor, where she had selected some ornaments worth about £13.00, she then queued to pay but there were customers ahead of her. She decided to try and pay downstairs, with a saleslady with whom she had generally dealt, but as she descended the escalator she saw that she had a number of customers around her as well. No one had every questioned her integrity, particularly in her own country where she occupied an important position, and foolishly she decided she would cross the road to the bank which she had used during her visit, change her dollars and return and pay for the goods. As she reached the pavement, a lady store detective challenged her, asked her to return to the store and called the police, to whom your client gave her explanation of having intended going to the bank before returning to the store.

Thus, you are faced with a typical set of facts such as constantly recur with slight variation and almost inevitably result in a conviction. On further questioning you learn that because she was in a hurry she had arranged for a car hire service, which she had frequently used, to have a taxi waiting for her at 12 noon at the back of the store, and she had been arrested at 11.50 a.m.

You commence your analysis of the case, or in military terms, your appreciation of the situation. Your primary object is to secure an acquittal; your subsidiary objects are bound up with the second phase, namely, the factors which affect the attainment of the object. What are these?

(a) The vast majority of shop-lifting cases, whatever the mitigating circumstances, are properly charged and justly convicted. Magistrates tend to become case hardened, always hearing the same story, and store detectives know what the magistrates expect to hear. The second object is to convince them that this case is the exception rather than the rule.

(b) The store detective will, as likely as not, be an experienced witness and you have no material with which to refute her evidence or confound her. Can any be found?

(c) Your client had just enough money on her to pay for her purchases and a great deal more in dollar currency. This, however, is a common feature in many shop lifting cases, and cannot greatly assist.

(d) The sole issue in the case is whether the client was leaving the shop having stolen the articles or whether she intended to return and pay as she contends. That will be decisive. What then are the factors involved there?

I. Against her account:

(i) She did not at once say she was going to the bank and returning to pay.

(ii) She knew she had not paid for the goods when she left the shop.

(iii) She told no one before leaving what she intended to do.

II. In favour of her account:

(i) She had a taxi waiting at the rear entrance. If she was making a getaway she would more easily have dashed into the taxi and departed.

(ii) When stopped she was about to cross the road in the direction of the bank.

(iii) She told the store detective and the police officer, on the latter's arrival what had been her intentions.

(iv) She was of excellent character and standing.

(v) The bank revealed on investigation that no one had made inquiries as to whether she was known there and changed currency there.

The next stage of the analysis is to decide the courses open to the defence and the prosecution. The defence must call the taxi driver to prove he was waiting for the accused at the rear of the shop. Two strong and preferably impressive witnesses should be available as to her character. The shop must be viewed in advance of the hearing to familiarise oneself with the layout. If possible, someone should be called from the bank to prove she was known to change currency there. The prosecutor should be asked whether there are any facts which are unknown to you. (Having done this, you find there are no fresh matters.) Moreover, there do not appear to be any courses or opportunities open to the prosecution which are not customary.

The Plan

You, therefore, make your plan.

There is no real prospect, on the commonplace facts, of persuading the magistrates that your client is clearly innocent. Your objective, therefore, is to persuade them that they are left with a doubt as to her guilt, which means they must acquit. Subject to anything unforeseen which may emerge, you will ask only a few questions of the store detective and police officer.

The essence of your tactics must be to impress the bench into accepting that your client acted foolishly and not wickedly; and the fact that she was proceeding in the direction of the bank, and not in the direction of the taxi, waiting at the rear of the shop, lends credence to her story. Elimination, as already stressed, being the key to sound advocacy, cross examination and argument should be limited to that one central issue.

Occasionally, unforeseen bonuses will accrue. In the case on which the above facts are based, the police officer proved to be young and inexperienced and in his evidence in chief described how he told the accused she had committed a crime by leaving the shop with goods for which she had not paid. It was thus possible to suggest that she had been charged without any regard being paid to the true state of her mind at that time and the need to establish a dishonest intent. The bench acquitted.

Of course, it will frequently occur that changes in the course of a trial will render it necessary for you to make adjustments to your tactical plan. Generally, however, the main lines of the plan can remain intact, and it is important in most cases, once you have decided upon the tactics involved, to endeavour to adhere to them. All of these considerations have equal application whether the case is being heard before a jury or before lay magistrates, a stipendiary magistrate or a judge sitting alone.

Subsidiary Tactics

A further tactical consideration is one which affects the overall conduct of the case. What is to be your subsidiary objective in regard to the effect which the presentation of your case is to have upon the court? Are you best served by trying to enlist the sympathy of the court? Or is it a case where you believe that such injustice is likely to result from an adverse decision against your client that the court can be aroused to a sense of indignation? Or is it a case where it is important for you to stimulate the inherent sense of injustice to which every court endeavours to respond? If your objective is to win sympathy then your questions are probably better framed and your arguments advanced without any outward sign of aggression; you would appear to be presenting your case in a state of mind reflective more of sorrow than of anger. If you are seeking to arouse the indignation of the court at the position in which your client has been placed you will tend to frame your questions and your arguments with a certain degree of indignation on your own part. It is hardly necessary to say that, in all respects, moderation in argument and approach tends to be better received in English courts than other methods of presentation.

Once you have determined which are the essential aspects of your case and the manner which you can best present them you will need to give careful thought to the laying of the best foundation for cross-examination and subsequent argument. It is never wise, for example, to put your important questions directly to a witness in cross-examination, unless it happens to be a witness who you have decided is anxious to agree with you and to help your client. In the common place example of the shop-lifting charge given above your primary objective, as we have seen, is to satisfy the court that your client may well be telling the truth when she says that she intended to go across the road to the bank to change some money and return to pay for the goods. If you put to the store detective that your client was walking across the road or in that direction in order to go to a bank where she could have changed money, you will at the worst get an answer to the effect that this was not so or, probably, at best, that she had no idea where your client intended to go.

Laying a proper foundation necessitates dealing with the questioning in a wholly different way. You would first ask her whether there is in fact a Barclays Bank on the side opposite from the shop. Since you know there is such a bank there, and the probabilities are that the witness will as well, she will necessarily confirm that fact. Next you might ask her whether she was present when the police interviewed the defendant; again you will have gathered from your client that this was the case. You will remind her that your client had said she was going to the bank to cash some money. Since the police were then present she will doubtless agree with that. You might then ask her whether she had been to the bank to see whether the defendant was known there. You have previously ascertained that no such enquiries had been made.

There is a psychological aspect to such a question. The store detective will suspect that the question may indicate a course which perhaps she should have followed and had failed to do and this may well condition a desire not to be unhelpful to you in the line of questioning you are following. The next minor objective therefore is to get the prosecution witness to concede before the court and thus implant it in the mind of the justices, that there was a strong possibility that the client's account was a true one. If therefore you simply ask her whether she agrees that the client was probably going in the direction of the bank, perhaps in order to change money she will justifiably reply that she has no idea about that and in any case the defendant did not say this to her when she first stopped her. If, however, your last question on this aspect of the matter is: "You of course are not able to dispute the possibility that this lady was intending to go to the bank?" you will probably get an answer that she cannot contest it and you might conclude by saying "and when you stopped her outside your shop she was facing towards the opposite side of the road and was walking towards the kerb."

This simple example, it is hoped, gives some indication of the sort of pre-thinking which is necessary in laying a tactical foundation even for the most commonplace cross-examination.

Anticipating the Witness

It also illustrates the importance of making an intelligent appreciation of the witness's likely answer to any of the questions you are minded to put. Bound up with this is the need to determine which is the best time at which to ask particular questions or to advance particular points in the presentation of the case. It is also a well recognised psychological fact that when laymen are called as witnesses for one side or the other there is a tendency for them subconsciously to ally themselves with the side which calls them. They will often feel they now have a duty to support the side for whom they appear. They will also tend, therefore, to believe that anyone who cross-examines them is trying to destroy their side's case. You will often as a consequence need to ask some fairly innocuous questions on peripheral matters in order to win their confidence and establish the belief that you are not trying to trick them. If having tried that method of approach you still find the witness difficult, unco-operative or aggressive obviously you must then resort to alternate means.

No hard and fast rules are available to guide you but, as a general principle, it is better only to put your important questions or points when you have already demonstrated to the court by earlier questions the precise thesis upon which you are relying.

Impact on the Tribunal

A further important tactical consideration is the need at all times to assess and re-assess the impact which the witness or your questioning of him is having on the tribunal. If it seems that the court regards the witness as having been discredited it is often unwise to push your luck too far. To continue may often arouse sympathy from the tribunal in favour of the witness and diminish the good which you have already done in respect of your own case. Indeed, that brings out still another tactical principle of general application, namely, that it is never wise to pitch your objectives too high. If you have substantially achieved an objective it is better to leave well alone. Moreover in the general conduct of the case you should never seek to achieve more than the essential minimum to establish that which you have decided is necessary for the proper presentation of your client's case.

Tactical Positioning

As with military strategy, and many other pursuits, an important part of your function is to endeavour to anticipate and counter the likely tactics being employed by your adversary. Although not something which will frequently occur, a good example was afforded at an inquest.

The father of a deceased girl was seeking to establish that her death was occasioned by unlawful killing. A barrister was representing the father; application was made by another barrister to represent the remaining members of the girl's family and to this request the coroner somewhat unusually acceded. The two barristers then sought to position the advocate for the party (who they were suggesting might have been responsible for the death) between the examination by the first barrister for the family and the examination of the second barrister. Once this was drawn to the attention of the coroner and objection taken the carefully planned tactic was rendered nugatory by the coroner insisting that the two barristers thus appearing for the family, put their questions in advance of the other advocate. Thus, it can be seen, that where there is any choice permissible in regard to the order in which questions are put, this can be an important tactical consideration. It is often better to be able to put questions last in order to cover anything which might otherwise occur after the cross-examination has been completed. On other occasions, you may decide it is better to be the first to tackle the witness. Similarly, those responsible for drawing indictments or charges where there are a number of defendants frequently consider the tactical advantages for the prosecution in having the defendants in a particular order thus ensuring the cross-examination will probably follow that course. If there is reason to believe this has happened it is often a good counter-tactical move to try and secure the court's agreement to some departure from the order thus laid down.

Obviously it is impossible to catalogue all the diverse situations which can arise in the conduct of a trial or in the preparation for it and to suggest methods and means of dealing with each. What however has been written may well be sufficient to indicate the degree of thought which has to be given to every possible and foreseeable aspect of the conduct of the case; the need to give careful thought as to how to deal with any of the tactical activities of your adversaries and the fact that conducting a case is not something which can be approached without the most careful consideration of all these many factors. Moreover, this is as true for the conduct of a simple case in the lowest court as it is for the conduct of a complex case in the highest tribunal.

IV: Presentation in Court

A certain proportion of the cases in which you are instructed will, in due course, come on for trial. In criminal causes the proportion will be high, since, from their nature, once instituted they are difficult to halt. Indeed, where the prosecution abandons a case, it is customary for the court to refer the matter to the Director of Public Prosecutions so that he can be satisfied that the case is properly abandoned and that he ought not to take it over and continue the prosecution. In civil cases, however, as the Judicial Statistics show, not more than one or two per cent. of the process issued results in trial. Indeed, in some ways, the test of a sound legal adviser is to be found as much if not more, in the extent to which he compromises litigation on terms acceptable to his client, than in the extent to which he succeeds at a trial.

Appearance in Court

It is not intended to dwell at great length upon the question of how you will dress when you are appearing in court. Common-sense clearly dictates that you will be neat and tidy. In a popular television programme the participants sought to suggest that the requirement that those appearing before the court, particularly defendants or parties, should be in a presentable form of dress, was an unjustified requirement. Good manners, which one hopes remain important, clearly require that those who attend the Queen's courts, should, as a matter of courtesy, present themselves in a neat and tidy fashion. There is, however, more in it than this, so far as the advocate is concerned. It is simple psychology to which I have already alluded that people are predisposed to accept the opinions of those whom they like and to reject those put forward by persons whom they dislike. It is no part of the technique of persuasion to appear in court in such a fashion as may tend to antagonise the judge or at least irritate him upon your first appearance. A court of law is not the place to establish your reputation as a sartorial trend-setter. Err, in the interests of your client, on the side of caution. Neat, conventional attire cannot, and will not, offend anyone. It may be true that Charles the First and his subjects wore colourful garb under long flowing locks, but he still lost his head. You are paid to retain yours. The recent change in the law which will afford some solicitors equal rights of audience to that of barristers will unquestionably give rise to other questions affecting dress.

Indeed, it is regrettable that consideration has not been given to this matter, as it already affects those courts where equal rights of audience have long existed. The adversarial system which we employ requires, at least in theory, that, as far as is practicable each side should be evenly represented. If one side appears by a barrister dressed in one kind of gown and wearing a wig more in keeping with the seventeenth century, whilst the other side has only a bareheaded solicitor dressed in a different sort of gown but which appears to be similar to that worn by the court usher, where stands the theoretical fairness of the system?

It should not be thought that this is a mere quibble. Some years ago I appeared on behalf of a defendant at Bow Street Magistrates Court in a revenue case. The revenue was represented by a barrister employed in that Department, the magistrate, was also a barrister, but he had only recently been appointed and knew neither my opponent nor me, and, of course, we were both unrobed. At that time counsel sat in a bench to the left of the magistrate; solicitors at a bench in front of him. Because the case involved a vast quantity of documents and the table at the solicitors bench was much larger than that at the counsel bench, my adversary suggested we change positions to which I agreed. As the committal proceedings continued and I, occasionally, raised procedural or evidential objections, the magistrate uniformly upheld them. When, after many days, the documentary evidence had largely been adduced, my adversary suggested we might resume our proper places. We did so. From then forward, such objections as I advanced were almost uniformly overruled. It is of course possible that my earlier objections were more valid than my later ones; there is also another possible explanation.

It must be desirable that advocates of whichever branch appear in the same form of attire and address the court from the same bench as one another. Anything else seems indefensible as much from a psychological as an equitable point of view. Lawyers in other jurisdictions find it odd that silks are placed in a pre-eminent place in our courts, once more upsetting the balance of the adversarial system.

When the new procedures are introduced these defects may, it is to be hoped, be remedied; perhaps the time may now have come to abolish wigs, with the approach of the twenty first century; the Lords of Appeal in Ordinary seem to manage very well without them.

Punctuality

Into the same category falls the necessity for punctuality. It is not generally a propitious start to the presentation of a case to arrive at court to find the judge has had to adjourn because you were not present. It is no better if you arrive just as the judge is sitting so that you must feverishly endeavour to put your papers into order. It is at this moment that they disappear onto the floor as you flurry around your place, and it is hardly calculated to endear you to your tribunal if the first view you present of yourself is a rather shiny patch on the back of a skirt or a pair of well-worn trousers.

Knowledge of the tribunal

There are also other advantages in arriving at court in good time. I have previously indicated the desirability of finding out in advance of the commencement of your case, as much as possible about the tribunal before which you will appear. If I am appearing in a magistrates' court with which I am not familiar, I always make it my first task to inquire from the usher, the police, the clerks, such colleagues as may be in the court, or anyone able to assist, as to who will be sitting on that particular day, and, in a lay magistrates' court, the occupations of the particular lay justices. There are a variety of reasons underlying this pursuit. Your case, for example, may be concerned with medical matters, and one of the bench may be a doctor. All the more reason, in that event, to take care that you do not put forward any medical propositions which will clearly be unacceptable to him. Similarly, the subject-matter of the case may fall particularly within the province of the trade or occupation of another member of the bench to which the same observations apply. You may discover that the members of the bench, as so often they do, reflect varying degrees of intellectual training and attainment. You want to present your case in such manner as is clearly intelligible to the meanest intelligence on the bench, and yet not so over-weeningly simple that you will insult the intelligence of the better intellectual ability upon it. Further, it is often useful in the course or argument to be able to draw upon similes which will be readily understandable to your tribunal, and in a court consisting of laymen there is nothing better than to be able to demonstrate an argument by reference to something which is known to a member of the bench as part of his daily occupation. On the other hand, it is bad and dishonest advocacy to endeavour to create some wholly unjustified rapport between the bench and yourself. I once heard a speaker telling law students of an occasion when he had appeared before a bench, having discovered that a member of the bench had attended the same public school some years before he did. He contrived, there-fore, to mention in the course of his address the fact that he also had been at the same school. Not only does this reflect no credit on the advocate; not only does it offend the first rule of advocacy, namely that you are not there to project your own views or associations, but it is calculated to misfire. If the person to whom your remarks are addressed has that degree of intelligence which you should certainly attribute to him, he will know this type of advocacy for what it is, and be sufficiently disgusted to reject it and the rest of the advocate's arguments out of hand. In short, try to adjust your language and manners to suit those whom you are addressing. Do not address lay justices in high faluting legal language; nor judges of the High Court as if you were explaining a principle of law to a first year student; but do not imagine that you should ever in this process cease to be natural and yourself. I know of one advocate, who typifies too many, who is most able but has not achieved the distinction which his ability deserves, because it has been said of him that he talks up to those above him and down to those below him. On the other hand, because judges sitting in the High Court or above would, for the most part, not be there unless their ability, experience, integ-rity and sense of fairness was beyond question, do not regard them as other than human beings with all the frailties, quirks, prejudices and other personal peculiarities. A good judge recognises his own short-comings and overcomes them; certainly he strives manfully—and in these days womanfully as well—not to show them. As an advocate, bear in mind that they may still be lurking underneath.

Your task as an advocate practising the technique of persuasion is to learn, in advance, as much about those you need to persuade as can possibly be known. Enquire of your more senior and experienced colleagues before appearing in front of judges unknown to you; they always make it their job to know what particular judges do or do not like. To have asserted to a certain Lord of Appeal in Ordinary, now deceased, in the course of argument, that fox-hunting was a wicked and cruel pursuit could be likened to relying on a judgment, in argument, of Mr. Justice Kekewich, which it was once said, was like starting out in a boat on a Friday: unfortunate whilst nor necessarily fatal. Certainly, few senior practitioners would have fallen into such error.

Similarly, never allow yourself to feel intimidated. The vast majority of the judiciary, at every level, will sense inexperience and be anxious to assist and encourage you. Understandably, to the young they seem rather like gods. A few of them fervently share this opinion with you; your task is not to disabuse them, but knowing their weakness to turn it to advantage. The oldest practitioners have had time to glance under their desks at their clay feet.

It would be foolish, in this context, not to recognise, however, that when solicitors begin to exercise the wider rights of audience there will be some judges—few in number, perhaps—who will be less than co-operative. Those who vigorously opposed the reform—as some of them did—will be happy—albeit unconsciously—to demonstrate how calamitous the decision has proved to be.

Whether you are a solicitor facing such a judge or a very young barrister undertaking your first case before one whom your colleagues have with due politeness designated "difficult," there is one infallible answer. If you have mastered your case, facts and law, and present it clearly, concisely, confidently and courteously, there is nothing which the most difficult of judges can do which is not likely to recoil in his own face.

If you are appearing before a tribunal rather than a court of law, try to ascertain in advance the degree of informality which the chairman prefers. Some chairmen believe the maximum of informality to be desirable. Tribunals were established for settling disputes in relation to money claims, such as pensions and housing, which affect many lower paid citizens, in the belief that the quality of justice would be improved by an informal approach. Experience has shown that, save in the more simple cases, this is not necessarily correct, however, it is unwise to adopt a method of conducting your case which differs from that which the tribunal prefers.

Finally, in this connection, these guidelines have equal application to juries. Simplicity and clarity, giving explanations where appropriate and eschewing any hint of a patronising approach are evident in the most successful addresses to a jury.

Preparation in court

A further and final advantage in being in court in good time is that it will enable you to ensure that your client is present; that he has with him all the documents which you required him to bring (assuming some have been left in his custody); that you are satisfied that all the exhibits are available and in order; in a motoring case that your client has brought with him his driving licence, without which, in the event of a conviction, the case cannot be concluded in a criminal court. Punctuality will enable you, or those to whom you have deputed the task, to provide the usher, as previously indicated, with a list of the authorities, if any, which you are going to quote to the court. In the time before your case is called, you can also endeavour to re-assure your client and your witnesses. As likely as not, this may be their first appearance in a court of law; they are likely to be worried and agitated, and the manner in which they later give their evidence will be greatly enhanced if you are there to reassure them, and if you have cemented their confidence in the fact that you are there to assist them. You should, for instance, tell them what to call the judge or bench, and if they have not previously been told, by you or by others, exactly what will occur you should explain the procedure in simple terms. In preference, however, this should be done during the period of preparation of the case.

When you have entered court on time, you will be able to set out your papers in order and, what is equally important, set out the authorities to which you are going to refer in the order in which you propose to quote them. It is perhaps unnecessary to remind you that you will stand whenever you address the court; that it is neither good manners nor good judgment to address the court from a seated position. Even when you are not speaking, if the judge addresses some remark to you when you are seated, you will come to your feet as a matter of courtesy. When you first enter the court, and whenever you leave it or return to it, you will bow to the judge or the bench. If there is a form to be completed with your name and address, make sure that you complete it.

It is desirable that the judge should, if possible, know who you are. There is a story, old and probably apocyrphal, but nevertheless in point. A young and inexperienced barrister went into court and began to conduct his case. The judge passed a note to the usher reading, "Kindly ascertain for me, counsel's name." The usher made his way across the court and in a loud voice, which could be heard by all present, said to the young man, to his obvious embarrassment, "The judge says, what is your name?" "My name?" said the young barrister, "Oh, my name is Brown—and pray tell me," (in equally audible tone) "what is the judge's name?" This, however, is not a course of conduct to be recommended.

I make a point of marking in the top right-hand corner of the note book which I take with me the name of my opponent. I find that I have great difficulty, as some of you may do, in remembering names, and it can be singularly off-putting if one wishes to refer to one's opponent's argument and one cannot remember his name. It is convenient always to mark it in exactly the same place on your notes so that you can readily know the place where you will find it.

All of these matters to which I have referred may seem trivialities of such a nature as to be unworthy of mention. Those however, who have had no experience of court procedure can be very confused unless these niceties of appearance are within their knowledge. I make no excuse for having dwelt upon them here. In the same category, every practitioner can remember the uncertainty with which he addressed different tribunals when he first started out on his legal journeys. Needless to say a High Court judge is addressed as "My Lord"; a county court judge and a Circuit judge as "Your Honour"; a Recorder as "Sir," or, if addressing the jury or other third parties "the learned judge" or "the learned Recorder"; the lay magistrates as "Your Worship" or "Sir" or "Madam" (as the case may be); Metropolitan magistrates generally as "Sir" or "Madam" (they are entitled to be, although they are not usually, referred to as "Your Worship") a coroner as "Sir"; and the chairmen of tribunals similarly.

Although something might be borrowed from the technique of persuasion by addressing a junior police officer as "Chief Superintendent" it is not considered to be an advantage to address a High Court judge as "Your Worship" or a county court judge as "Your Lordship." Nor should you emulate the course I saw followed by one litigant, who called everyone in court, from judge to usher, "Your Majesty."

Addressing the court

Finally, be sure that you know your own case forwards and backwards so that you can, if possible, conduct it without reference to your notes; but, if that is not possible, at least ensure that you are fully familiar with every fact and point of law and authority to such extent that you cannot be faulted. Only hard work and labour can ensure this. Then, remember again that people are predisposed to accept the opinions of those they like and to reject those put forward by those they dislike. Thus, your general reputation for integrity and amiability, your courtesy and reasonableness must, and does, play a significant part in your success as an advocate. If you cannot be the sort of fellow whom people easily like then at least try to be the sort of fellow whom people respect.

The method of introducing yourself varies in regard to different tribunals. In courts of law, at all levels, *i.e.* the High Court, the Crown Court, county courts and magistrates' courts, it is customary when you first rise to your feet to announce that you appear on behalf of the plaintiff or the petitioner, and that Mr. Joe Snooks appears on behalf of the defendant or the respondent. If you are appearing before a planning inquiry, or the Lands Tribunal, you must first of all, if you are a solicitor, announce your name and address and if a barrister, your name and the name and address of the solicitors instructing you; whether you are a solicitor or counsel, and the names and qualifications of the witnesses you intend to call. If you have not finally decided who or how many of the witnesses you will call, you should announce that fact to the tribunal. In licensing applications it is also wise, having indicated to the committee that you appear to make the application, loudly to inquire whether there are any objectors to your application. If there are, they will come to their feet, give their names and the names and addresses of those for whom they appear. If on the other hand, you are opposing an application in a licensing matter, then you will, of course, announce that fact at a suitable opportunity, and give names and addresses of those you represent.

I have given these few particulars in the hope that it may ease your course when you first appear before one of these courts or tribunals. But the underlying principle involved is that you should make certain that you know the procedure of the particular tribunal before which you are going to appear. Indeed, if you know you are shortly to appear in an unfamiliar setting, it is wise to visit it in advance, to observe how those with experience conduct themselves. To demonstrate your familiarity with the procedure tends to inspire rather more confidence in your ability as an advocate than if you give the uncertain appearance of being a ship at sea without a rudder.

Presentation of the case

I do not wish to delay very long in dealing with such matters as the method of your delivery. The points which I would urge you to watch are:

   (i) clarity;
   (ii) simplicity;
   (iii) putting your points succinctly;
   (iv) developing them in an interesting way;
   (v) presenting them with integrity; and
   (vi) doing so without any trace of pomposity.

Despite all that is written in so many books on advocacy about the manner of delivery and address, and whilst I do not in any way wish to underestimate the importance of any of the six factors to which I have referred, I would put as the foremost in importance that of integrity. Your task will be to persuade the tribunal to accept the arguments and reasoning which you are going to place before it. It is true that the court must judge the case and not the advocate; it is correct that the case must be decided on the evidence and not on the personality of the lawyer, but when all has been said the fact remains that unless one advocate is more persuasive than another, in a large number of cases where the die might be cast either way the result would be an indeterminate decision. If you are known to be tricky, untrustworthy and unreliable, the court will need that much more persuading in the instant case that your arguments are sound and your facts fairly and truly presented. Never, therefore, put forward points of law which you know to be bad in the belief that your undoubted histrionic ability will hoodwink the court. If you succeed in doing so (and this is most unlikely) on one or two occasions, particularly if the decision is subsequently upset by a higher court, the judge will naturally tend to distrust you and your arguments on the next occasion you appear before him. Never distort facts to meet your case. Never—one hardly needs, one might think, mention this—engage in rudeness or impertinent remarks to your opponent or even to the court. Yet it is surprising the number of occasions in which one can sit in court and observe advocates, who should know better, address the court in an offensive fashion, presumably in the belief that they are doing some good for their clients.

Your task is to succeed for your client in accordance with the law; it is neither your right nor duty to win your case by any means, including withholding from the court decided and authoritative cases which would defeat your cause.

You must constantly keep your emotions under control. Never lose your temper, or you will assuredly lose your case, your dignity and your client.

Again, do not take advantage of your position as an advocate pointlessly or viciously to attack a witness. Never put in cross-examination allegations which you know to be unfounded—even if pressed by the client to do so. Far better that you lose your client than your reputation. If you lose one client others will take his place; if you lose your reputation you will lose your entire calling.

Eschew any declaration, hint or suggestion of your own beliefs or opinions. The court is not interested in what you consider to be the law—but what it is; it does not desire to have your opinion on the facts—but merely the arguments which indicate the possible interpretation and value of them.

You "submit" and not "opine"; you "suggest" and not "declare"; you "persuade" and not "assert."

Above all, do not be pompous. Many a young barrister has discovered twenty-five years after his call that he is left with little to show but his pomposity, and that the first essential of genius is humility.

A further sound precept is never to waste time. There will, of course, be occasions when you have a particular course to pursue, or a particular line of argument to present, and the court, not being informed at that stage as to the purpose of the course you are following, may understandably display impatience. There are certainly occasions when it does become necessary to pursue a particular line, although the court is obviously unwilling that you should do so. These occasions, however, will be rare. There is a world of difference, however, between taking necessary time when it is not your custom to waste it, and appearing to waste time when it is your invariable habit to save it. Observation shows that much time is wasted by inexperienced advocates from either a desire to prove how clever they are, or a misguided belief that no evidence adduced is so unimportant as to be unworthy of the fullest investigation. For example, in charges of handling under the Theft Act, evidence is adduced, usually in the form of statements, tracing the course of the goods from place to place in order to prove them to have been stolen. It may be tempting to cross-examine, although your client does not dispute that the goods were stolen, to show that the evidence of a witness who speaks to the dispatch of goods is inadmissible, because he was not present, or did not himself complete the consignment note. At best, you will necessitate an adjournment and delay while another witness is brought; at worst, you will antagonise the court whom you wish to persuade as to the innocence of your client. In either case you will have shown that you have not mastered the technique of persuasion.

Moreover, you should always bear in mind the wise advice of Lord Alexander, Q.C. who, when at the Bar, was one of the most successful advocates of his day: "Perhaps the most important key to the conduct of a case in court, which must never be forgotten, is that you are the advocate and not the audience. You have throughout to be asking yourself the difficult question "What is my hearer thinking?" This sensitivity to the tribunal requires flexibility."

The wisdom within this statement, however, is not as it asserts limited to conducting a case in court. It has no less application to every aspect of persuasion whether in court, at a meeting, whilst lecturing, speaking after dinner or pursuing any activity where you seek to retain the interest of an audience. The requirements for a court technique can be learned by watching others engaged in any of these activities. How often have you sat miserably after an indifferent meal and heard a speaker drone on long after he had lost his audience? He is clearly insensitive to what is in the mind of the audience. One can, after a time, learn something of the reaction of an audience from the expression on their faces; the extent of their attention to what you are saying; the lack of movement as they listen and, particularly with laymen such as might be found on a jury, a clear indication of assent to the proposition you are advancing. But flexibility remains important for sometimes laymen are seen to indicate assent when they may have misunderstood what is being said. If, therefore, you entertain any real and sensible doubt as to whether your argument has been understood and accepted, or if you believe part but not all falls into this category, you must be able and willing immediately to adjust your thought, so as to convey that part of your argument which might be acceptable in a form which it seems will be accepted.

If, moreover, the court itself indicates doubt as to your contentions, you must be equipped to determine at once whether you are safe to abandon that theme, or whether, by putting it another way, you may still prevail.

On the other side of the coin, it is right to point out that many of the matters which I have urged upon you are equally incumbent upon the court. Courtesy, dignity and integrity are as essential on the part of a court concerned for the due administration of justice and you are as much entitled to be treated with courtesy as the court is entitled to expect courtesy from you. If you do not receive it, it is proper for you to make a protest in suitable terms. It is no part of the duty of an advocate to give way to every whim and fancy of the court, and a courageous dealing with the affairs of your client—as long as it is done with due regard to the dignity of the court—will, in the long run, be commended by all who witness it.

The method and speed of presentation of a case will tend to vary depending upon the type of tribunal before which you are appearing. A trial in the High Court or a county court tends to move at a rather more leisurely pace than a trial in a magistrates' court before a stipendiary magistrate. I have sometimes heard it said that a case should be conducted in a magistrates' court with the utmost speed while the stipendiary is sitting, but should be taken rather slowly when lay justices are present. I believe this is the wrong way to put it. I prefer to say that all cases should be conducted with as much expedition as possible whether heard by a stipendiary magistrate or lay justices. It may however, on occasions, be desirable to deal with matters at rather more length, in terms of explanation, before laymen—in regard to matters of the law or facts which are especially complex—because they, of necessity, lack the training and experience of a legally qualified stipendiary magistrate.

Taking Notes

Before one comes to consider particular modes of presentation in particular courts, there remain one or two general observations which might usefully be made. In addition to a large note-book, you would be well advised to have with you a pen, and two coloured pencils, one red and one green. As you take a note of the evidence—which you should do quickly, accurately and fully—you should mark with the red pencil those passages of the evidence upon which you propose to cross-examine, the green pencil being used to underline those parts of the evidence which might be useful for reference when you come to your final address.

In taking your notes I would advise you to leave a large margin on the left in which you can insert a short pithy note, indicating the line of cross-examination you hope to pursue.

It cannot be too strongly stressed or too often repeated that the function of the advocate is to assist the court; and in this connection first impressions can be most important. It is true that a bad first impression may be corrected, but it is well to remember that a good first impression generally forms a solid basis for success. An advocate who is assured, orderly and clear, inspires confidence in the court. He represents a rock on which the court feels it can rest. A flustered and nervous advocate who cannot, at the right moment, find the pleadings or the correspondence is unlikely to create the sort of impression required to indicate that his cause is just and his arguments sound. Knowledge defeats nervousness; care begets confidence and knowledge, care and confidence all invite acceptance of the opinions which are being advanced.

Opening address

Let us now examine some particular facets of particular types of proceedings. In your early days, your civil works as an advocate will inevitably be in the county court. Your first course, if you are appearing for the plaintiff, is to open the pleadings. This involves no more than reading to the county court judge the various pleadings, commencing, of course, with the particulars of claim, then moving to the defence and so on.

Pleadings

Although, of course, more a matter for preparation than presentation, it will be convenient for me to mention here the need to prepare the pleadings with special care. In the county court, unlike the High Court, rather less attention is paid to the technicality of pleadings, and no claim will be allowed to fail merely because it has been inadequately pleaded. Abundant opportunity is generally given in these courts for the appropriate amendment so as to ensure that the claim is properly presented; sometimes a drastic amendment may involve an adjournment so that your opponent is not taken by surprise, and your client may, as a result, be ordered to pay the costs thus wasted. On the other hand, attention is paid by the judge to the way in which the case has been pleaded, and whilst this is not the place at which to embark upon any sort of instruction as to the preparation of these documents, you would be well advised to familiarise yourself with the essentials of this very important subject. A judge may, understandably be attracted to well prepared pleadings. It is a badge of competence, which renders him the more likely to assess the draftsman as an advocate upon whose assistance he may rely. As such it is an important part of the technique of persuasion.

Pleadings must state only material facts. If you include evidence or law you demonstrate, at a glance, your inexperience or ignorance. That Sam Jones asserted that the defendant was driving his car at 70 miles per hour round a bend, and lost control is the evidence. That the defendant drove negligently is the averment of fact, of which the particulars of fact might be, *e.g.* that he drove round a bend at an excessive speed, and, additionally, that he failed to exercise any, or any proper control over the vehicle. Moreover, you must limit your pleading to material facts, which are those alone which are essential to the plaintiff's cause of action or the defendant's defence.

The object of a pleading is to crystallise the whole of the issues of fact for determination, with a view to reducing the area of contention and thus saving time and expense. Indeed that is the fundamental of good advocacy itself.

For the young barrister, the drawing of pleadings is the bread and butter of his existence. It is also important that solicitors should master the essentials, and this will become vital as these rights of audience are extended. Not only must they prepare pleadings in the county court and even—in some cases the High Court, but they must be able to check, and where necessary amend, with the draftsman concerned, the work of counsel.

Above all, the experience which comes from analysing the issues which arise, the discipline which is instilled by the elimination of surplusage, which forms the basis of good pleading, and the legal research necessary to isolate the issues, provide an invaluable exercise in most of the basic essentials of effective advocacy. Nevertheless, there is need for a radical overhaul of the whole process of pleading so that an essential summary, not merely of the issues involved, but of the evidential substance of each side's case is disclosed at an early stage of the proceedings.

The Imaginative Approach

Remember that it must help your presentation if you can hold the interest of the tribunal by presenting your case in an imaginative and lively fashion. There will be a very large number of cases where this will not be particularly easy. A claim for the price of goods sold, for rent or for debt, in the ordinary course of events, can hardly be made to scintillate. But, from time to time, you will have a case involving some interesting point of law or an especially interesting aspect of fact, and it is as well at the outset to draw this to the attention of the judge in order that he, in turn, may share the anticipation of relief from the more pedestrian and tiresome types of litigation. In any event, always inform the judge at the outset, in one form or another, of the main legal problems which it falls to him to determine.

Having done this you will turn to the outlining of the facts, being careful to limit your opening to matters which you are sure you can prove. Having given the judge the gist of the case which you are presenting, you may endeavour to anticipate the nature of the case to be presented by your opponent—suggesting, perhaps, possible answers to his arguments.

It is difficult—and, indeed, dangerous—to lay down any hard and fast principles as to whether or not you should at this stage endeavour to present arguments as to why the contentions of your opponent are unlikely to be sustainable. You may, in doing so, limit yourself to a line of attack which is not borne out by your own evidence, or which, as the result of the failure of the defendant's evidence, is the subject of instant modification by him. This can be extremely dangerous in the technique of persuasion. On the other hand, if there is some particular aspect which is clearly the kernel of the defence, and if you are able to adduce clear incontrovertible evidence and solid argument against it, it can sometimes be quite effective to demolish this argument from the outset. What, however, is important is that, wherever possible, you should reach a decision on this matter before you go into court, and not make a rash, hurried—and probably incorrect—decision whilst on your feet.

We then come to a part of the opening address which I personally regard as the most vital of all. If you have followed the course which I have recommended you will have determined—and noted—at an early stage your own objectives in the case, and the matters which it is necessary for you to prove. This will, in turn, have required you to formulate the questions which arise for answer in the proceedings. It is therefore of the greatest possible assistance to the court if at this stage you say to the judge "Your Honour, in my submission, the questions which you will have to ask yourself when you have heard all the evidence are five in number, and are as follows. . . . " As likely as not, if the judge has formed the impression that you know your business, he will here interrupt you and ask you to dictate the questions to him, so that he can write them down. If he does, you may congratulate yourself upon having secured his confidence and having established a solid foundation upon which subsequently to base your arguments.

Magistrates' Court

Since the procedures are in no respects common to all courts, it will be better, I believe, if we now turn to the opening speech and procedure in the magistrates' court. You should make a point of ensuring before you go into court that you have familiarised yourself with the relevant sections applicable to the case which you have to present, or, if it is a common law offence, to the law. This is quite as important in the magistrates' court as in any other court. You will have examined the statute to see whether the offence is one which must be tried summarily; which must be tried on indictment, or is one in which you have to make a decision as to where you wish it to be tried and you will have discussed this with your client. You will have looked up the appropriate punishment, noting the section and reference in order to draw it to the attention of the court. This is equally as important if you are appearing on behalf of the defendant as for the prosecution, yet it is a constant source of amazement to me how often advocates appearing in these courts are to be found banking on assistance from the clerk on these matters, rendering it clear that they have not given any attention to those points whatsoever.

Election for Trial

Much thought should be given to those cases in which, on behalf of your accused client, you have a right to elect for trial by jury or to leave the case to be dealt with summarily in the magistrates' court. The problem is eased, although never wholly solved, if you have special knowledge of the court. A difficult point of law may be better argued in a higher court than before a particular clerk to the justices whom you may not regard as being especially bright. It should be said in fairness, however, that there will equally be cases where such a point of law is more likely to be appreciated and correctly adjudicated upon by the clerk to the justices than by a particular recorder or Circuit judge. In general terms the clerks to the justices do a superb job, and the fact that there are as few appeals from decisions of justices as there are is largely to their credit. Once again, however, it is proper to point out that this sometimes depends upon the skill with which the case stated is drafted or amended by the clerk—sometimes, in the result, bearing little relation to what actually went on in the magistrates' retiring-room or during the hearing.

That, however, is to digress, and this particular decision as to venue is one which involves the application of psychology in its most accurate form. One develops (or hopes one develops) a sixth sense as to the way particular facts will react upon magistrates in general or one in particular, and how they are likely to be received, by comparison, if placed before a jury. A good example is to be found in the now more rare—but formerly frequent—charge of driving whilst the ability to drive is impaired through drink. Magistrates tended to become case hardened about the defences advanced in those prosecutions. As a result the probabilities were that before the magistrates the accused would be convicted; on the other hand juries were more prone to the view that "There, but for the grace of God, go I," and acquit. In those circumstances the tendency of the experienced advocate was to elect for trial and, where these cases are still brought, that practice equally applies today. If experienced in dealing with this problem one must endeavour to stand aside, as it were, from the case, dispassionately scrutinising evidence which will be adduced by the advocate on behalf of his client, and ask oneself the question "Is this account more likely to be accepted by a stipendiary magistrate, lay justices or a jury at a higher court?" Only when you have answered this question to the best of your ability can your decision be made. That decision, however, must be the decision of the client; all you can do is place before him the various pros and cons: the prospects of success; the chances of greater or less punishment; the cost and delay. Explain the situation to him as best you can, advise him; and ask him whether it is his wish, in the circumstances, to be dealt with summarily or on indictment. Do, however, pay due regard to the greatly increased cost involved and the possible waste of court time which may arise, from an election for trial. Of necessity, the decision is one for the client, but you have no duty to encourage election for trial for inadequate reasons.

Outline of Facts and Law

There has been an increasing tendency (in consonance, I regret to say, with an ever-increasing degree of laziness in the presentation of cases in all courts) to avoid opening the facts of a case, the advocate merely contenting himself with stating that the facts will reveal themselves when the evidence is called. If statements have been served under the provisions of the Magistrates Courts Act 1980 there may well be justification for this course. Similarly in truly simple cases it may be acceptable. On the other hand, under the system which currently operates, the defendant may have little knowledge of the case which he has to meet; his advocate will probably have no real opportunity of deciding how he should tackle the witnesses in cross-examination, and unless you tell him at this stage upon whom you are proposing to rely to prove the different facts, he may needlessly duplicate his cross-examination. With this in mind, therefore, in fairness to the court and equally to your opponent, it is proper in a large number of cases shortly to open the case giving an indication to the court and your opponent of the way the case is likely to develop and the salient facts to which each witness will speak. Once again, it is vital—perhaps more vital in criminal proceedings—to open the case only on facts which you have reason to believe you can prove. Do not allow yourself to become embroiled in sententious language condemning the conduct of the defendant, or expressing your opinions as to the degree of severity of the offence charged. This is no part of the duty of an English prosecutor; his duty is merely to present the case to the court with equanimity, with fairness and integrity in order that a proper decision may be reached. If you are addressing lay justices it is generally wise, at the outset, to explain the law to them in fairly simple, but not dreary, terms and if addressing a jury to explain the issues which arise for decision, or, where you are defending and the Prosecution has previously outlined these, those issues to which you may wish to direct particular attention. If you are addressing a stipendiary magistrate do not address him as if he were a lay justice. He probably knows the law better than, and certainly as well as, you, but if any unusual section is involved you are well advised to refer him to it; similarly, whether it be lay justices or stipendiary magistrates, in a case which involves anything out of the ordinary, no harm is done by indicating to them the questions which they will have to answer at the conclusion of the evidence. Whether you are addressing lay justices or a stipendiary, speed and efficiency are the keynotes, although as I previously indicated you may be well advised to go into rather more detail, albeit in simple terms, when addressing a lay bench.

Reacting to the facts

Whichever the court, before which you are to appear (whether a higher or lower court) there is an aspect which is worthy of special mention.

You will have formed your own view as to the facts, and will have determined at an earlier stage the theory which you will try to persuade the court to accept as being the most acceptable to your client. The fact that the case is being contested necessarily means that your adversary sees, and will present, the facts in a different light. The judge or jury may see them in a still different light from either of you.

It is important, therefore, to stand back and ask yourself, divorced from any previously conceived notion, how a particular judge or jury is most likely to react to the facts. As experience grows one becomes better able, though by no means infalliably, to gauge such reactions, but common-sense can carry you a long way. For example, in a libel case, although it may be tolerably clear that there has been a technical libel, the surrounding facts likely to emerge are such that the claim may be rejected because the judge or jury will form an adverse opinion concerning the plaintiff, or because they find the behaviour of the defendant newspaper to have been objectionable. Juries and lay justices and even judges, do not have a different reaction from that which affects them in the pursuit of their daily affairs, nor do they become endowed the moment they enter a court of law, with greater or different intellectual powers from those which they otherwise possess.

Many experienced advocates make it their practice when in doubt, to outline the facts to a spouse or a friend and seek their reactions to them, knowing that, as likely as not, this will be the same reaction as is likely to evidence itself in the tribunal.

Both those exercising judicial office and juries are concerned to do justice, not to be bound, necessarily, by the technical legal requirements, and may well be influenced by considerations of disgust, sympathy, compassion or any of the other emotions which can beset the best of us. Judges, as can be seen, are more than reluctant to decide cases in favour of a party who has the letter of the law on its side, but who's case has little to commend it on the merits.

It is your task, having dispassionately evaluated the facts, to present your case from the opening to the closing speech in such manner as may steer the tribunal away from such initial reactions as they may entertain to that which you may advance in your conduct of the case, or alternatively to turn their pre-conceived ideas to your own advantage. The more subtly this can be achieved the better.

The Opening

In a good opening of a case, one can detect the golden thread—namely the need for elimination—which runs through all sound advocacy. Avoid stilted and outmoded phrases. The advocate who tells the court—as some barristers feel constrained to do—that "the facts fall within a very small compass" should recognise that the use of such phrases shows that his compass is already affected by local magnetic disturbances, and his client should enter the court with a lifebelt round his neck.

What is required is a concise epitome of the essential facts; a short summary of any defence revealed by the facts elicited by the investigation; a succinct statement of any especially cogent reasons why the advocate's case appears more probable than any other possible version, and a brief but accurate account of the legal principles involved, where these are not already obvious.

In complicated cases the opening may need to be long, but it should never contain more than is essential to bring the mind of the court to the law and issues which it must determine. Before a jury, a competent advocate will be seen to do no more, save that his presentation may be in simpler terms, couched in the form of a homely or dramatic story. Simplicity and conciseness should certainly be the keynotes.

For years, the myth was fostered that some peculiar and God-given ability was essential to present a case to a jury, which is not to be found even amongst those able to give a clear and good account of themselves before judges or any other group of people. For example, solicitors, it was said, were unequipped to address juries, although for years they had been addressing lay justices, company shareholders and voters as prospective candidates as well as the House of Commons, when elected. This myth was exploded, when solicitors, who had previously been excluded from addressing a jury, proceeded to sum up the facts to juries, as well, and sometimes better than the advocates who had preceded them. Presumably, the same thing was said of Lloyd George, the Welsh solicitor, whose oratorical powers contributed to his soubriquet of the "Welsh Wizard."

Whether you are a solicitor, or a very young and inexperienced barrister, do not be intimidated by the outworn mystique which has been built around the task of addressing a jury. Compared with addressing some of the Judiciary it is childs-play, assuming of course you have prepared your case as you should have done. The essentials are not one whit different from other forms of advocacy, bearing in mind that, within the guidelines, which I trust have emerged, you will give special weight to simplicity, clarity and the other obvious considerations which arise.

Indeed, when one sits in court, watching others address juries, those who have done their homework soon shine above the remainder, and too often, the cause for concern is how much better it could have been achieved. To take only one example, the jury is usually swimming in wholly unexplored waters. The meanest advocate knows they must be told what the case is about; that they must duly trot out that they alone are the judges of fact and that His Lordship, or His Honour, is the judge on the Law; that the onus of proof lies on the Crown, and that they have sworn truly to try the case. How much, in this day and age, all this "legalese" is really necessary may be questioned, but it is the custom. What however you more rarely encounter, is any endeavour by the average advocate to analyse, for the jury, in simple terms, the areas of contention, which guides them towards the questions and considerations which will assist them to elucidate the problems.

Examination-in-chief

Whichever be the court before which you are appearing, you have now reached the stage at which you call the evidence. In civil proceedings it is customary to call the plaintiff first. There is, however, no hard and fast rule about this and you may, if you wish, call your witnesses in such order as seems to you to enable your case to be presented to its best advantage. In criminal proceedings by reason of the Police and Criminal Evidence Act 1984 if you intend to call two or more witnesses to facts including the accused you must call the accused first, subject to the discretion of the court. Although, therefore, the order of calling the witnesses is otherwise a matter for you, once a witness is in the box he should tell his story chronologically. So far as possible, he should be left to give his own evidence, since, as you know, you are not allowed to put leading questions in evidence-in-chief. If you detect undue nervousness on the part of the witness, commence by asking questions with which he can easily deal, such as the nature of his employment, until he is at his ease. There is, however, more to examination-in-chief than meets the eye, and it is desirable at all times that the witness should remain under your control. Merely to say "Will you now tell your story?" or "Will you now give your evidence?" is not sufficient. Experience shows that the witness who is left to tell his own story does not—and that which he tells becomes a tangled skein. Take him up to the essential points and only then leave him to give his account, taking care to interrupt (although not so as to put him out of his stride) in order to bring him back under control so as to maintain his account precise and chronological. Phrase your questions simply and shortly, and take care to put only one question at a time. It is a useful exercise to take proofs of evidence and quietly, in the privacy of your own room, endeavour to ask a series of questions, as in the examination-in-chief, employing the shortest and simplest terms to achieve this end.

Leading Questions

Although you are not allowed to put leading questions, you may in general terms do so:
   (i) in respect of introductory matters—such things as the name, address and description of your witness;
   (ii) as to matters which are clearly not in dispute; and
   (iii) to secure an express denial of an allegation.

We are not, however, here concerned to study the law of evidence although you should certainly do so. However, perhaps two examples of leading questions, and how they may be removed from that category, might be helpful. It is clearly a leading question, *i.e.* one which suggests the answer to the witness, to ask, "When Mrs. Brown approached, did the accused raise the knife?" Yet those new to advocacy experience great difficulty in re-phrasing such a question so that it is not leading. Thus, it still remains a leading question to ask, "Did the accused raise the knife, or not, as Mrs. Brown approached?" Those words still, as you will note, suggest to the witness the answer which is required. In fact, in order to avoid a leading question, you may have to ask a series of questions. It might, therefore, be done in this fashion:
   Q. "Did you see Mrs. Brown?"
   A. "Yes."
   Q. "Was anyone else present?"
   A. "Yes, the accused."
   Q. "Where were they in the room?"
   A. "On either side of it."
   Q. "Did they remain there?"
   A. "No. The accused went towards Mrs. Brown."
   Q. "What, if anything, happened then?"

A. "He raised a knife."

Another exercise with which you will be frequently faced is where a witness fails to come up to his proof, a failing to which, you will find to your chagrin, too many witnesses are prone. The proof of evidence may state "As I arrived at my home, I saw the defendant standing on his doorstep in his pyjamas." When you ask, "As you arrived at your home, did anything unusual occur?" you may get the surprising answer, after a worried pause, "No." You cannot correct this, if it is an important contested fact, by saying, "Did you not then see the accused in his pyjamas?" Instead you must proceed something along these lines:

Q. "You have told us you saw the accused when you left work on the Thursday morning?"
A. "Yes."
Q. "How was he then dressed?"
A. "As he is now—in a suit."
Q. "Have you ever seen him dressed otherwise?"
A. "Yes. In his pyjamas."
Q. "When did you see him dressed in his pyjamas?"
A. "When I came home from work on the Thursday."

Please do be careful, moreover, when examining-in-chief—or for that matter in cross-examination—to avoid peculiar mannerisms which can become annoying to the tribunal. Do not, for example, repeat—as do some advocates—the points the witness gives. The court will have heard the answer for itself, and if it has not done so it will ask the witness to repeat it. Echoes may be fascinating in the Tyrolean foothills, but they are tedious in a court of law.

A witness may refresh his memory by referring to any writing or document which he made, or, if made by another, which he saw and examined, contemporaneously with, or so soon after, the event, as to be virtually so. A common example is a police officer's notebook.

It is for the court to determine whether it was made sufficiently contemporaneously. So, before allowing your witness to refer to it you should ask him whether he has such a record, whether he made it himself, and how long it was made after the events it purports to record.

If the first opportunity which the witness had to make it was some hours after the event, this may suffice.

However, merely refreshing his memory by looking at the document does not make it, or its contents, evidence; but if the witness is asked to read it, or part of it, aloud, that which he reads becomes evidence. This shows the need for caution. It is wise to see the document yourself before the witness refers to it (you may also ask to see it before cross-examining the witness). If the part you might wish to put in evidence contains other material damaging to your case, you might decide not to adduce it since your opponent can then ask for the damaging part to be put in evidence as well.

When examining-in-chief in cases of sexual assault do not overlook that, contrary to the normal evidential rules, you may adduce the hearsay contents of the complaint, provided it was made at the first reasonable opportunity and was not made in answer to questions of a leading, threatening or inducing character. Such evidence, however, does not establish the truth of the complaint so proved, but goes only to show consistency between the complainant's conduct and the evidence, or to negative consent, where that defence is relied upon by the defendant.

The evidence which you adduce must, of course, conform with the Rules of Evidence. For example, you must not introduce hearsay. Perhaps, the commonest error amongst tyros is to ask "What did Mrs. Jones then say to you?" thereby hoping to elicit what is, in effect, the evidence of someone who is not to be called: hearsay in its purest form. The practice has grown up, over many years to overcome this difficulty, by saying to the witness: "I do not want to know what Mrs. Jones said to you, but what did you do as a result of what she said to you?" Judge Michael Hyam, in his excellent book "Advocacy Skills" points out, as is, of course arguable: "This formula is objectionable because what was said may be inferred from what the witness did. If what was said was relevant, it was hearsay, and if it was irrelevant it was inadmissible anyway." He quotes the case of *Glinski* v. *McIver* [1962] A.C. 726, as the authority for that proposition, and, indeed, the words which he quotes were words of Lord Devlin in that case.

It may be desirable to offer a few comments on the Judge's contention. First, the remarks of Lord Devlin would seem from the report to have been made *obiter dicta*; no objection had been taken at the trial to the form of the question, and the evidential arguments had not been fully canvassed, if at all. Secondly, the so called device, being the form of the question, has achieved such a degree of usage, that it is unlikely that a court would now exclude it, as is the case with other circumstances in which the hearsay rule might otherwise be excluded but are now admitted. Thirdly, the argument appears to involve a high degree of sophistry; it is largely a question of semantics. If the witness were asked "Did you have a conversation with Mrs. Jones?" and then, "What did you do next?" the hearsay rule would not be breached, since the argument wholly turns on the consequential nature of the question, but the inference would still be drawn. Finally, in some respects the question has become academic. Since the passage of the Criminal Evidence Act, 1962, in civil proceedings, the witness can actually be asked what was said by Mrs. Jones, if notice is given of the intention to ask it, and no counter notice is received, although this is not the case in criminal proceedings.

On balance, I would still be inclined to continue with the well established form, unless the connection between what was said and the consequential action was crucial to the outcome of the case, as it might possibly have been in the case quoted, had objection been made at the time it was first put. This, however, does help to demonstrate that it is important for you to be familiar with the above quoted Act, with the Criminal Justice Act, 1988, which is helpful in regard to the admission of documentary evidence and with the provisions of the Police and Criminal Evidence Act 1984, many questions concerning which arise in the course of trials.

It is also invariably better to bring out any point which may be adverse to your case in examination-in-chief, rather than leave it to your opponent to bring it out with greater effect in cross-examination. There are numerous excellent books on evidence and examination-in-chief to which you will refer, and I do no more than give you the barest of introductions here.

Cross-examination

We must therefore now turn to cross-examination, it being assumed that whilst your opponent's witnesses

111

have been giving their evidence, you will have been taking the fullest possible note in your note-book in the way already suggested.

There is perhaps no aspect of procedure more subject to abuse than that of cross-examination. The young advocate tends to believe that this is the point at which he can and is expected to display all his finest histrionic talent. The fact is, however, that the first question which you should ask yourself before you cross-examine any witness is "Need I cross-examine at all?" It can perhaps but rarely occur, but unquestionably it does occur with rather more frequency than you might imagine, that it becomes wholly unnecessary to cross-examine witnesses at all. If they have said nothing which harms your case, the pursuit of cross-examination may achieve no more than to elicit an answer which will. Moreover, if you can present your arguments on the basis that you accept the evidence which your opponent has adduced but that you are able to place a different interpretation on it, you are immeasurably nearer to a favourable result than in presenting a case involving facts which the courts must first determine by reconciling or rejecting the version of one side or the other. Elimination and selection are the two keys to effective practical cross-examination.

This having been said, it remains your duty—in cross-examination—to put to the witnesses your client's case, and in particular every disputed fact, so that they may have the opportunity of dealing with them. Moreover failure to cross-examine implies acceptance of the witness's testimony. It is this principle which lays stress on the desirability of underlining in red those parts of your notes of the evidence in chief, on which you propose, and more particularly, need to cross-examine. A common trap for the tyro—and too often for the experienced—is to forget in the intensity of the pursuit, to cross-examine on an aspect which is in dispute. Later when he is addressing the court he will bring his opponent to his feet to remark "there was no cross-examination on this issue."

If the omission is crucial, it may be necessary to obtain leave for the witness to be recalled so that the disputed facts may be put to him. Usually, an apology by the offending advocate will be accepted, but that does not alter the fact that the evidence in question might effectively have gone unchallenged.

Unlike evidence in chief, you may put as many leading questions in cross-examination as you wish, but, remember, that even then those words which have not been put into the mouth of the witness carry greater weight.

Make a point, therefore, before concluding your cross-examination of glancing back through your notes to ensure that every essential disputed fact has been covered.

It is especially at this point that your earlier analysis and listing of objectives will stand you in good stead, since you will long ago have set down, noted and have available, the only matters which need to be put to the witnesses called by your opponent, in so far as they have not meanwhile been admitted on the pleadings, by formal admission or in earlier evidence.

Is the Question Necessary?

If, however, you have earlier elicited from the witness—or a different witness—an admission which assists your case, do not, in your understandable enthusiasm, put the same or a similar question again; you may well get a different answer which nullifies the good which your earlier question achieved.

Not only, therefore, should you always ask yourself at the outset, "Need I cross-examine at all?" You should throughout your cross-examination, when once you have decided to embark upon it, repeatedly ask yourself, "Need I cross-examine further on this or any other point?"

An excellent example of this principle occurred in a case tried on Assize. An accused—represented by a young barrister—was said to have had unlawful intercourse with a young girl. The principle witness for the prosecution was an old farmer, who was said to have observed all that had occurred from an adjoining field. The cross-examination proceeded in this fashion:

"Mr. Jorrocks, I take it, when you were a young man, you sometimes went out with girls?"

"Oh! yes. Oi did."

"And sometimes you would walk with one in a field?"

"Oh yes."

"And sometimes you both might sit down on the grass?"

"Yes, that be roight."

"Now tell us, Mr. Jorrocks, did it not sometimes occur that whilst your girlfriend was lying back on the grass, you would lean across and give her a kiss?"

"Oi, that be roight."

Relentlessly the young barrister plunged forward.

"Mr. Jorrocks, do you think that anyone observing you thus, from an adjoining field, might have thought you were having intercourse with her?"

"Thats so," said the witness, and after a short pause, "and what's more, they would 'ave been roight."

How disastrous and unnecessary was that last question which elicited such a devastating reply. How much better to have left it and to have invited the appropriate inference in the final address, when no one (except, perhaps, an unkind judge) could have gainsaid it.

Allied to the need to keep a cross-examination as short as possible is to ensure that it is always directed to significant points—with an objective—and never aimless. Time and again one sees advocates—and I regret to say not only young ones—who appear to be asking questions because they wish to be seen earning their fee, or because they have forgotten how to bend their legs in order to sit down.

"I put this to you, Mr. Snoggs . . . " and "I put that to you, Mr. Snoggs . . . "—aimlessly and monotonously they and the legal aid drift on, whilst everyone knows that Mr. Snoggs has already said the contrary and will continue to deny it—thereby underlining his own evidence. Cross-examine only to establish your previously determined objectives or to break down some specific and known contention of your opponent or to ensure, as you must, that you have put your case to the witness to enable him to deal with it. I would dearly like to know how many questions are daily put in cross-examination by advocates for no better reason than they are, at the same time, cross-examining themselves as to what on earth they can next ask the witness which might be to some effect.

Questions from the Bench

Do not be resentful of questions put by legally trained minds from the Bench. Human nature being what it is, an answer which is elicited in furtherance of your case by the judge himself is likely to appeal more to him (and his ego—since he has one as well) than a number of answers elicited by you. If, however, and it will not, I trust, too often be your own unhappy experience, the judge interrupts so much that he is in danger of taking the cross-examination out of your hands and, as was once said of a High Court judge by the Court of Appeal, "has so descended into the arena as to have got mixed up in the dust of the conflict," then take a firm line. Such an occurrence might provide the rare—and very rare—instance when a little—and very little—gentle sarcasm may be justified. "Would Your Honour feel it amiss if, at this point, I put a question to the witness, even at the risk of breaking into Your Honour's prolonged—and wholly effective—cross-examination?" The use of such tactics, I stress, can rarely be justified. Sarcasm seldom achieves anything but the raising of resentment; rudeness achieves still less.

If, however, in order courageously to present your client's case, you are constrained from sheer necessity to resort to something which might be thought to be sarcastic or even slightly rude, make sure you are wholly right. To be rude and wrong is fatal and, it has been cynically said, is a privilege exclusively reserved to the Court of Appeal.

Cross-examination as to Documents

Similarly, hesitate long before putting questions in cross-examination to which you do not know the answer, or without having a fairly shrewd idea of what it is likely to be. On occasions you may have to do so. The most effective cross-examination is likely to result when founded on an irrefutable basis, and the witness's own correspondence or documents are the best examples. However, do not put such documents at once to the witness. If he at first commits himself to something different from the contemporaneous record he will demonstrate his unreliability. Thus:

"You have told His Honour that in June of last year, you had no intention of selling the house?"

"That is so," says the witness, "I had no such intention."

"Your mother-in-law was living with you in June of last year, was she not, Mr. Twists?"

"Yes."

"Her name, I believe, is Mrs. Tango?"

"It is."

"I want you to look at the letter which you wrote to my client on the 30th June. . . . "

The letter is handed to the witness and he is required to read a statement which it contains, over his own signature, that he must sell the house at once as Mrs. Tango is getting increasingly irritable and he must find somewhere to live away from her.

There are witnesses who will find a way around such a dilemma, but cross-examination which proceeds from such a firm base as this is by far the most effective. Always, therefore, search the documents and correspondence for such opportunities. Judges, you will notice, always rely more on written contemporaneous records than the spoken account of transient recollection.

Impeaching the Reliability of Witnesses

In many cases you will, of course, not have such documents available to you. There are a large number of criminal cases, for example, in which documents play a very small part. Apart from the need to ensure that you put to the witnesses for your opponent every disputed fact and your own case, your cross-examination will largely be directed to impeaching the credit or reliability of the witness under cross-examination. There are a number of ways of doing this, but you must judge each case upon the basis of the material which you have available, and the type of witness with whom you are dealing. For example, you might try to draw the witness into giving an account which is contrary to that given by other witnesses on his own side or to reliable witnesses whom you have called or intend to call.

It is often helpful to draw upon facts which are established beyond doubt, for example the day of the week, or a television programme which was showing at a particular time, in the event that a witness has said that he was watching television. It is often useful to search out underlying details of a statement which he has made which are themselves capable of proof beyond doubt, and which differ from the account which he has given.

Whilst the desire to be succinct in the phrasing of your questions in cross-examination should generally be paramount, there are many occasions, particularly with this type of cross-examination, where you must bide your time. A mere frontal attack upon the witness with a single question is unlikely to be successful. Thus, merely to say "is it not a fact that you were watching a detective film on television at that time?" will unquestionably produce a negative answer if he has already said the contrary. It is wholly legitimate in this pursuit to engage in something of a battle of wits. Before you come to your crucial question, you should direct a series of questions to the witness designed to make him dubious as to his own recollection and uncertain as to what material you have to disprove what he is asserting. For example, you might ask him who was with him when he was watching television. If he pretends to be unable to remember you might then ask him whether it is not the fact that his brother and sister-in-law were there, and mention their names. You would then question him as to what he was doing immediately before and after the vital time when the television programme was supposed to have been shown. Thus, by going round the various points, and avoiding, for the moment, the specific matter to which your attention is really directed, you may cause him to have doubts as to whether or not his recollection of this particular vital point is correct.

This apart, it is seldom of value to cross-examine down to meticulous details unless they are in truth vital. This is only calculated to exasperate the court and to waste time. Moreover, by this degree of circumlocution you may create a situation in which the court is unable to see the wood for the trees.

When cross-examining self-assured or authoritative witnesses—especially experts—it is often wise to do so in a spirit of compromise rather than aggression. If you vigorously press a witness so as to require total capitulation in relation to the retraction of a statement you may achieve nothing. Psychology is again as important here as in seeking to induce a court to change its mind. No one likes to be shown to have been wrong. Find, therefore, some acceptable means of getting the witness "off the hook" without undue loss of face. Thus in putting a contrary view do not seek his direct agreement with the proposition "you accept your earlier view was wrong?" Rather, edge him towards your own objective with:

"Would you accept, there can be two different views on this matter?"

"Yes."

"On reflection, do you feel that that which I have put to you is, at least, acceptable?"

"Yes."

"And, in the light of your reconsideration of the problem, perhaps, even preferable?"

"Possibly so."

I once saw the late Sir Patrick Hastings cross-examining a witness in an important case. At a crucial moment in the directing of his questions, he noticeably paused and searched laboriously through his papers. At last—with evident relief—he found the paper for which he was searching. He continued his cross-examination with the paper in his hand—but without mentioning it. Every answer then given by the witness suddenly became favourable to Sir Patrick's clients' case, whereupon he put the paper down on the desk, without having produced it. The paper was then seen to be blank.

Rules of Evidence

It is wholly desirable that you should equip yourself with a sound knowledge of the law and rules of evidence. No amount of knowledge of the technique of questioning can make up for a lack of understanding of the rules which cover the admissibility of evidence. To take an example, which has already been noted: it is a rule of evidence that if part of the contents of a written document is produced then it is open to the opposing party to require the remainder of that part of the document to be adduced. This rule therefore underlines the dangers of cross-examining as to part of the contents of a written document if the remainder of it may be likely to damage your own case. In such circumstances it is better to omit references to the document altogether; or at least, if the document will in any event be adduced in evidence, to present it in its entirety rather than leave your opponent to destroy a point made from part of it. Similarly, if you wish to rely upon part of a written document to support your case, it borders upon insanity to spend another part of your time attacking (as I have seen some experienced advocates do) some other aspect of the document. All you will achieve is to demonstrate the general unreliability of the document, and to that extent dilute the value to be placed upon the part upon which you seek to rely. None of these propositions involves earth-shattering discoveries. They are all self-evident if given a modicum of thought, and yet it is quite surprising the number of advocates who do not appear to have given the slightest attention to these manifest truths. Do familiarise yourself with procedure by studying the rules of the appropriate court to the point of clearly understanding them. I remember being somewhat nonplussed by a young advocate who strenuously endeavoured to re-examine the witnesses after cross-examination by an advocate for the second defendant, and before I had cross-examined for the second defendant. When duly corrected his next endeavour was to prevent me cross-examining the first defendant after he had given evidence against my client.

Attacking Prosecution Witnesses

Another pitfall in cross-examination—in criminal cases—is to attack the witnesses for the prosecution without having first satisfied yourself that your own client has a good character. The Criminal Evidence Act of 1898, with which you will be familiar, has the effect of putting your own client's character in issue if you impeach the character of a witness for the prosecution. Nor is it safe to rely merely upon your client; it is another cause for surprise how often clients will mislead their own lawyers about their previous good or bad character and how often the lawyers will fall into the trap. Before the cross-examination begins, and for preference before the case begins, ascertain from the prosecutor whether or not he has any record of any previous convictions of your own client.

What, however, if you know that your client has previous convictions; that by cross-examining the witnesses for the prosecution you will put his character in issue, but the necessary conduct of the defence, on the basis of instructions given to you, inevitably involves an attack upon the prosecution witnesses? You would be well advised, in that event, fully to familiarise yourself, as best you can, with the law applicable to this particular course of action. The law in this respect, despite the decision of the House of Lords in *Selvey* v. *D.P.P.* [1970] A.C. 304, is far from satisfactory or clear. Your client is clearly on risk (except perhaps on a charge of rape) even where the casting of imputations on the character of the prosecutor is necessary to enable the accused to establish his defence. If you ensure, however, that your questions are limited, in attacking the prosecution, to those matters which it is vitally necessary for you to traverse in order to set up the defence, it is very unlikely that a court, which has an unfettered discretion in the matter, will hold your client's character to be in issue. There are those who—in the current climate for law reform—favour the ever widening of judicial discretion in such matters. It seems to be insufficiently appreciated that the more that discretion is enlarged the harder it becomes for the practitioner to know precisely how to conduct his case.

You, in the honest exercise of your best judgment, may believe that you have not gone so far as to impugn the characters of the witnesses or, if you have, not so far as to justify the discretion being exercised adversely to your client. The judge or court may think otherwise and you may find that unwittingly you are held to have put your client's character in issue. The only general precepts which can be advanced for your assistance are (1) never impugn the character of the prosecution witnesses unless you are convinced that no alternative is open to you; (2) if you have decided that such an attack is inevitable, limit it to those matters which are essential to raise your client's defence; and (3) although you know your client has convictions, take the greatest possible care to ensure, by inquiry from the prosecutor, their exact nature, since you may otherwise place yourself in an impossible situation. If, having decided that his convictions are such that the risk is justified, you discover too late that more serious matters of greater moment, in the context of the case, are recorded against him, you can cause irreparable damage to your cause. This having been said, there are the exceptions which make every rule and there will be cases—not frequently but occasionally—where, having decided that you must make the attack, you must needs go on and make it in a full-blooded manner, regardless of the consequence of putting his character in issue. One final word, perhaps, might be added on attacking witnesses; never, if it can humanly be avoided, engage in a dog-fight between a number of defendants, one of whom you are representing. If one sits in court watching criminal cases being conducted it soon becomes evident that the easiest way to secure the conviction of two or three defendants jointly tried is for each to launch an attack upon the other.

The Opening Question

You will often be well served if you take special pains to prepare your opening question in cross-examination. This is the moment which the untruthful witness has probably feared. He has not yet had time to adjust himself to your forensic ability, or lack of it, and a question which puts him off his stroke can be such that he may never recover from it. Perhaps the best—and certainly the most celebrated—example of this technique is to be found in the opening questions of the cross-examination by Lord Reading when, as Sir Rufus Isaacs, Attorney General, he prosecuted Seddon for murder, in the only murder case in which that celebrated advocate ever appeared. Seddon was a hard, avaricious, mean, tyrannical and unsympathetic insurance superintendent, who, it was alleged, had poisoned his lodger, a Miss Barrow, for no better reason than to get possession of a small amount of money which she possessed. Having filched it from her, a fact which he could not deny, Seddon had then had her buried in a pauper's grave. The Attorney General's cross-examination started as follows:

"Miss Barrow lived with you from July 26, 1910 to September 14, 1911?"

"Yes."

"Did you like her?"

This question had Seddon utterly baffled. The prosecutor repeated the question, but Seddon never fully recovered his composure. He was intelligent enough to know that if he said that he liked her he would then be asked why he had had her buried in a pauper's grave; on the other hand, if he said he did not like her, he was beginning to establish a motive for destroying her.

One is often asked by law students and young practitioners whether one can give any guidelines as to the way to cross-examine a particular witnesses. Needless to say this is an impossible task, since each witness must be judged in the light of the material you have available and the assessment which you have made of his veracity and intelligence. However, there are a certain limited group of witnesses for whom you may well develop a special technique.

Cross-examination of Police Officers

Police officers tend to rely heavily upon note-books or statements which they have previously taken. The courts must rely upon the accuracy of certain parts of their evidence more as a matter of expediency than as a result of any solid belief that what they are relating is fresh and accurate in their own recollection. Quite clearly, police officers who deal with a multitudinous variety of cases in the course of a year could hardly be expected to carry every detail in their minds, and must therefore rely upon contemporaneous notes which they should have made at the time, or the statements which they took. Any intelligent police officer must therefore know that it would be impossible for him to give evidence at all unless he had read his notes before he came into court and refreshed his memory. The only other alternative in the less serious cases is for him to refresh it from his notes while he is in the box. Similarly the same intelligent officer would know that the probabilities must be that he and his colleagues will prepare their notes together. This, however, generally extends to such lengths that the notes in the notebooks of different officers in the same case are identical to the last word. It is again something to which one could never really become accustomed on any basis of logic or common sense. Many police officers, however, will repeatedly deny any suggestion of collusion of this sort with their colleagues, and will seek to pretend that their evidence is based upon a clear personal recollection at the time they are giving their evidence, and that it is not dependent upon their note-book or other research. Although courts tend to rely more upon the general picture reflected by the officer's evidence and to pay little and insufficient attention to cross-examination directed to these matters it must be something which indicates the degree of reliability of a witness. Since, therefore, you will be unable to destroy an officer's evidence upon the basis that he cannot remember without his notes, where it is really necessary to challenge his evidence on such details, you will have to attack the notes themselves. To this end the officer will be asked when the note was made, and the time he was occupied in making it; whether it represented the whole of the conversation which he had with the accused. If it did not and he has omitted part (as invariably will be the case) you might cross-examine him, on the basis of your instructions, as to other things which the accused is alleged to have said to which the officer has attached little or no importance.

It will usually emerge that the officer, who has perhaps had a conversation with an accused person for anything up to an hour, will have then made a note of that conversation three or four hours later in a police station without the accused being present. It is quite inconceivable, in those circumstances, that he could remember the exact words of the accused down to every phrase and syllable. Nevertheless, there are sometimes officers who will assert that this is the extent of their recollection. It is a useful way of demonstrating to a court—particularly to laymen and presumably to a jury—the unreliability of such evidence to ask the officer whether (if he is in charge of the case) he sat through the evidence of Mr. Brown, the first witness to be called. If you saw him sitting there you are at no risk in asking this. You might then ask the officer whether he is able to repeat word for word, only two hours having elapsed since them, what Mr. Brown had said. Clearly he cannot, and it is therefore equally clear that his pinning of the accused down to a particular word or phrase is not something upon which great reliance can be placed.

Cross-examination of Expert Witnesses

A second category of witness is the expert witness, be he medical, scientific, or skilled in some other discipline. Expert witnesses are a much maligned body of people. It is true that some of them may be charlatans, but for the most part they are people who are concerned to give help to the court upon the basis of a life-time's experience and training, and moreover, training within a particular field. Nothing is to be gained by endeavouring to bully them (or, for that matter, any other witness). Although your object may often be to show that the extent of their knowledge and experience is less than the expert whom you propose to call, this needs to be done with a degree of tact and judgment. You occupy a powerful position in court in relation to an expert. To make him look silly (if you are able); to cause him to be the centre of your ridicule (if you are competent to do so), are not only unkind and unnecessary pursuits but may damage him in the pursuit of his own profession by destroying his reputation. Experts for the most part are dealing with matters which can be the subject of differing opinions. If the subject-matter of their evidence is something of scientific exactitude, then you are unlikely to get very far with cross-examination in any event. You should therefore endeavour to raise new facets or approaches to the problem which they have to consider and endeavour to persuade them that if the facets which you are putting to them are accurate then the conclusion which they have reached would have to be modified or changed as a result. I can illustrate this by quoting from the evidence in chief and of two witnesses in cross-examination in an actual case. It is an ordinary pedestrian cross-examination of medical witnesses in a set of not too difficult facts. The accused was charged with causing death by dangerous driving, and cross-examination of the two medical witnesses at this inquiry was directed to showing that the cause of death was not the driving but some other cause. The deceased was a lady of advanced years who had been a passenger in a car with which the car of the accused had collided. The doctors' evidence was as follows:

"I am a registered medical practitioner. On May 7,——, I was the house surgeon on duty at the M—— Hospital."

"A Mrs. X was referred to me then by the casualty department for admission. Mrs. X was identified to me by Mr. L. I examined Mrs. X. She was rather deaf. She complained of pain in the right chest. There was tenderness in the right chest. An X-ray revealed a fracture of the eighth and ninth rib on the right side. I saw Mrs. X again on May 10 and I diagnosed that she was suffering from a stroke, with paralysis of the right side. She developed a chest infection. Mrs. X later died, and as a result of something which I was told, I referred her body to the coroner for post mortem examination."

Cross-examination then proceeded as follows:

    Q. "How old was Mrs. X?"

    A. "Mrs. X was 87 years old."

    Q. "What was her condition when you first saw her?"

A. "She was conscious."

Q. "Did she remain conscious throughout?"

A. "No. When I saw her on May 10 she was in a coma."

Q. "Apart from pain on the right side, were there any other symptoms?"

A. "No."

Q. "When she went into a coma did you form any view as to the likely cause?"

A. "Yes. I thought that she had suffered a cerebral thrombosis."

Q. "Would I be right in thinking that the X-ray showed that the ribs had not penetrated the lung?"

A. "Yes."

Q. "And that there was no evidence of any fluid having penetrated the lung?"

A. "Yes."

Q. "You would agree that under normal conditions it would be unlikely that there would be any direct connection between a cerebral thrombosis and a fractured rib?"

A. "I think it would be difficult to connect the two."

Q. "When did you first detect the existence of a chest infection?"

A. "There was a chest infection when I examined her on May 10."

Q. "You found nothing to indicate any continued pressure on the lung?"

A. "No."

Q. "Neither on clinical examination nor on X-ray?"

A. "No."

Re-examined:

"Where there is thrombosis or haemorrhage the patient is prone to chest infection. I would not definitely say that a rib injury is a cause of thrombosis and chest infection. This lady, Mrs. X, was not in a state of shock when I first saw her on May 7,——. She was then clinically well. Her blood pressure was high."

The next witness was a pathologist whose evidence in chief was as follows:

"I am a doctor of medicine, M.D., PH.D., M.C.PATH., D.M.J. P.C. A—— identified to me at D—— Mortuary the body of Mrs. X."

"I performed the post mortem examination. She was a fairly well nourished elderly woman with a slight bruise beneath the chin, a bruising of the right upper chest and bruises of the legs being consistent with having been caused by a car dashboard. There was no fracture of the skull but there was an extensive left sided cerebral infarction. "Infarction" means death of brain tissue due to impaired blood supply. The vessel on that side of the neck supplying blood to the brain was considerably narrowed due to degenerative change. There was a transverse fracture of the middle of the breast bone and the frontal ends of the eighth and ninth right ribs were also fractured, consistent with a crushed chest. The lungs showed changes of basal bronchial pneumonia. The heart showed changes of chronic high blood pressure with advanced degenerative change in the blood vessels. In my opinion, the cause of death was bronchial pneumonia due to cerebral infarction and a crushed chest was an associated cause."

Cross-examination then proceeded as follows:

Q. "You have told us that the deceased had bronchial pneumonia?"

A. "Yes."

Q. "And also that there was evidence of a cerebral infarction?"

A. "Yes."

Q. "It is not uncommon to find bronchial pneumonia developing consequent upon a cerebral infarction?"

A. "No. It is not uncommon."

Q. "Indeed, cerebral infarction is not an uncommon condition in a woman of 87 years of age?"

A. "Indeed not, it is a common condition."

Q. "And if, as you have told us, bronchial pneumonia often follows cerebral infarction this also is a strong possibility for a woman of 87?"

A. "Yes. It is a common condition."

Q. "The chronological sequence would normally be cerebral infarction followed by bronchial pneumonia rather than the reverse?"

A. "Yes."

Q. "And was so in this case?"

A. "Yes."

Q. "The fracture of the breast bone and the frontal ends of the eighth and ninth ribs would be unlikely to have caused cerebral infarction?"

A. "The only part which the fracture would have played, if any, in the death would be in impairing

126

the breathing after bronchial pneumonia had developed."

Q. "You have described the fractures as having been caused by the crushed chest?"

A. "Yes."

Q. "So that there should be no misunderstanding about this, bearing in mind what was revealed by the X-rays and clinical and post mortem examinations, the crushing would have been momentary?"

A. "Yes, this is so. There was no permanent crushing. It was only at the point of impact and was a momentary thing which would have been released immediately."

Q. "This would indicate that the crushing, so-called, was very slight?"

A. "Yes. The degrees of crushing were nothing excessive as shown by the absence of bruising of underlying tissues."

Q. "You have agreed with me that the fractures were unlikely to have caused the cerebral infarction. What, in your opinion, would have accounted for the cerebral infarction in a woman of 87?"

A. "I would have accepted that the cerebral infarction was a natural spontaneous development."

By the Court:

Q. "Would the fact that the deceased had been involved in a car accident not have been a factor in her subsequent condition?"

A. "Had the degree for shock been severe enough to cause a fall in blood pressure sufficiently only to cause clotting and thereafter a possible cerebral infarction, I would have considered the interval of time between the accident and the cerebral infarction to have been a matter of hours."

Cross-examination resumed:

Q. "We have been told by the previous witness that when this lady was admitted to hospital on May 7, —, she was not in a state of shock."

A. "Yes."

Q. "In order to make this clear, it is of course clinical shock you mean?"

A. "Yes."

Q. "This is a different meaning from shock in ordinary parlance as when one speaks of someone having a fright?"

A. "Oh indeed it is. It is a severe condition."

Q. "As you have indicated, for clinical shock to be sufficient to clause clotting there would have to be a substantial fall in blood pressure?"

A. "Yes."

Q. "We have also been told by the last witness that on admission the blood pressure of the deceased was high. Is this not contra-indicative of any connection between the accident and the subsequent development of the blood clot?"

A. "Yes. If her blood pressure was high when she was admitted then there was no connection between the accident and the subsequent development of the blood clot."

Q. "This lady was admitted to the hospital on May 7 and did not die until on or after May 10. You stated that even had she been in a state of shock sufficient to cause clotting you would have expected the interval of time between the accident and the cerebral infarction to have been a matter of only hours."

A. "Yes."

Q. "Certainly not three days?"

A. "No."

Q. "This, then, would be another indication negativing the possibility of a connection between the accident and the cerebral infarction?"

A. "Yes."

There was no re-examination.

In the circumstances a submission was felt proper that there was no case to answer as this lady had died not as the result of the dangerous driving, but due to natural causes. This submission was upheld and the case against the accused dismissed, thereby saving the time, trouble and expense, let alone the anxiety, of a trial at the higher court.

If you examine this cross-examination, the technique involved becomes self-evident. It consists of putting a slightly different interpretation upon the known facts in order to induce an expert witness to accept a different hypothesis. Of course, this does involve either some limited basic knowledge of medicine if it is a medical

128

witness, or science if it is a scientific witness. This can best be done by enlisting the help of some other expert in that field and obtaining from him the necessary data upon which your cross-examination is to be based.

Cross-examination of Partisan Witness

How does one cross-examination a highly partisan witness; one who sees his task as supporting, at all cost, the party calling him. In the first place you must endeavour, as with all witnesses, to assess him, as he gives his evidence-in-chief. Manifestly, to be over-partisan itself indicates some error of judgment on his part. Is he, however, wickedly intelligent, incredibly stupid or merely dis-interested or misinformed on his subject? Here is one useful tip. This kind of witness will sometimes be predisposed to refute any positive statement which you put to him, on the assumption that, since you are putting it to him, it must assist your case and must, therefore, be denied. If, therefore, you phrase your question so as to suggest the opposite of what you require, he may unwittingly assist you. If, wishing to establish that it was fine on Thursday, you put to him "you will agree it was fine on Thursday" he will probably reply "no, it rained" or "I cannot recall." If, however, you ask "Is it correct that it was *not* fine on Thursday?" he may well reply that it was, adding that he clearly remembers. This example is an over-simplification but it illustrates the technique.

As a further refinement where you judge that his enthusiasm for your opponent's case is wholly excessive you may then seek to push him so far along the road of improbability that no court could possibly place reliance on his testimony. Let us take, as an example, an actual case heard in the county court. An old lady, around 70, sued a road making contractor for damages for personal injury sustained when she fell into an unlit hole in the highway. She had fallen at 9.05 p.m. and the defendants called a pleasant, but unintelligent, labourer with a broad brogue, to testify that he inspected the hole shortly before 9.00 p.m., when it was well lit. The end of his cross-examination ran rather as follows:

Q. "You came on duty on this Sunday at 8.00 o'clock?"

A. "Yes."

Q. "You normally work on Sundays?"

A. "Yes."

Q. "Commencing at 8.00 o'clock?"

A. "Yes."

Q. "Did you light the lamps?"

A. "No, they were lit before I arrived."

Q. "Was anyone else on duty with you?"

A. "No."

Q. "Did anyone come to the site after you arrived."

A. "No."

Q. "So no one other than you could have dealt with the lanterns?"

A. "No."

Q. "When were you first asked about this incident when the old lady fell into the hole?"

A. "About two weeks ago."

Q. "By whom?"

A. "A solicitor."

Q. "This incident happened nine months ago?"

A. "Yes."

Q. "Why do you say it was just before nine when you visited the hole?"

A. "I remember."

Q. "Are you required always to walk round the site when you are on duty?"

A. "Yes."

Q. "At what times?"

A. "Usually, about three-quarters of an hour after I come on duty."

Q. "But not always?"

A. "No."

Q. "It is because it is usually 9.00 o'clock when you walk around that you say that was the time on this occasion?"

A. "Yes."

Q. "You are sure that, just before nine, there were lighted lanterns round this hole?"

A. "Yes."

Q. "How many?"

A. "About three."

Q. "Might it have been four?"

A. "It could have been."

Q. "Or even five?"

A. "Possibly."

Q. "Or more?"

A. "Perhaps."

Q. "All alight?"

A. "Yes."

Q. "You heard the police officer give evidence?"

A. "Yes."

Q. "He said he walked past the hole at 8.50 p.m. and there was only one lantern, but he cannot recall whether it was alight or not?"

A. "Yes."

Q. "And that only one unlit lantern was found after the accident?"

A. "Yes."

Q. "So that between 8.50 p.m. and your arrival at least two or three extra, and perhaps, more lighted lantern were put round the hole?"

A. "Yes."

Q. "You did not put them there?"

A. "No."

Q. "And no one else, you have told us, was with you or on duty?"

A. "No."

Q. "Can you suggest how they may have got there?"

A. "No."

Q. "Do you think perhaps they were put there by leprechauns?"

A. (with a grin) "I don't think so."

Q. "And having put them there that these little chaps then took all but one away?"

A. (laughing) "I doubt it."

If the witness is not only obstructive but highly intelligent, to boot, the task is, of course, much more difficult. You may have to vary your approach between sweet reasonableness and simulated aggressiveness. You may have to content yourself with putting your client's case to him. If you can find written records, or contemporaneous letters to confound him you must use these to the full. In general, you are more likely to persuade him to put his account too highly than to induce him to accept that your client's version is right and his wrong.

Inquests

It is important to remember—contrary to the belief of many lawyers—that no right exists at a coroners inquisition to cross-examine the witnesses. The rules enable you only to examine them as to relevant matters which are how, when and why the deceased died. Your questions should be limited to matters which assist the enquiry and not to discrediting the witnesses. Some times the rules may be disregarded if the coroner does not intervene. Similarly, since you have no right to address a coroner's jury you may have to word your questions, until the Coroner stops you, so as to convey to the jury what you hope they may agree is the proper verdict.

Re-examination

I turn now to the question of re-examination. Its object is to explain ambiguities, qualify admissions, or to put answers, given in cross-examination, into proper perspective. As with examination-in-chief, no leading questions may be put. Moreover, the re-examiner may not introduce any new material—at least, without leave of the court—and if this is given as to a matter which was not adduced in evidence-in-chief, the opponent will be given the opportunity of cross-examining on the new material. Its effectiveness is often underestimated and as often dissipated. The ability to re-examine depends primarily upon having observed with sufficient care the evidence given in cross-examination; and having made suitable notes so that you may be assured as to which points must be covered. It is not, any more than any other forms of court activity, an occasion for wasting time. Re-examination should only be directed to really important and essential matters which have emerged to your disadvantage in cross-examination. The fact, however, that new material cannot be introduced does not mean that one cannot re-introduce facts which have not previously been canvassed, so long as they are related to the main purpose of that part of the cross-examination.

As before, the technique is perhaps best illustrated by an actual example. In an accident case the defendants' chauffeur had been driving a car, and it was his negligence which was in issue. Both sides had believed that he was alone in the car when the accident occurred, but it subsequently transpired that this was not so.

The cross-examination of the chauffeur had proceeded as follows:

Q. "Then you have nothing beyond your own story to support your version?"

A. "No."

Q. "That is very unfortunate. You were, I presume, alone in the car?"

A. "No. My employers' son was with me."

Q. "Indeed. And yet you are not calling him to support your case."

The defendants through inadequate preparation having learned for the first time of the son's presence, it was decided to call the son. He was only seven but he gave a simple and natural account which supported the chauffeur.

The child was then cross-examined:

Q. "Is the chauffeur a friend of yours?"

A. "Not very much."

Q. "I suppose you have talked about this accident since it happened, quite often to the chauffeur, haven't you?"

A. "No, I haven't."

Q. "What, have you never talked of it to him?"

A. "No, I don't think I have."

A moment's pause, when the child volunteered:

"My brother is a friend of the chauffeur."

Q. "He is, is he?"

A. "Yes, a great friend."

Q. "And your brother has talked about the accident to the chauffeur many times, I suppose?"

A. "Yes, he has."

Q. "And then, after your brother has talked about it with the chauffeur, your brother has talked about it with you, hasn't he?"

A. "Yes, he has done so."

End of cross-examination.

Re-examination.

Q. "How old is your brother?"

A. "Three."

This demonstrates re-examination in its most effective form. A question in the following form, "In cross-examination you told my learned friend that you were not in the vicinity of this public house on Friday, June 12? Is that correct?" represents the least effective way of re-examination. If one cannot do better than that, one is better not to re-examine.

Order of speeches

Having arrived at the time for the final speeches, it behoves you to familiarise yourself with the order in which those speeches will take place. A distinction needs to be drawn between civil cases and criminal.

High Court and Crown Court

The order of speeches is to be found in Archbold's Criminal Pleading, Evidence and Practice in relation to criminal proceedings—and in the Rules of the Supreme Court as it affects civil proceedings in the High Court. It seems unnecessary to repeat them at length here.

Civil Cases

In civil cases there will first of all be an opening speech by the plaintiff, who will then call his witnesses. If no evidence is then adduced for the defence the plaintiff will give a final address, to which the defendant has a right of reply. If, however, the defendant calls witnesses, then after the plaintiff has opened the case and called his witnesses, the defendant may open his case; he will then call his witnesses; there will then be a speech made for the defendant, and a reply given for the plaintiff. In the county court, however, if only one speech has been made for the defendant, either on opening or closing his case, the plaintiff will have no right of reply except by leave of the judge. But county court judges have a special discretion as to the order of speeches and you should inquire as to the practice in a particular court.

Criminal and Domestic Cases

On the hearing of an information in the Magistrates Court the order is as follows: the prosecutor opens the case and calls evidence for the prosecution. The defence may then address the court or make an opening address, but will be allowed no other speech without leave. If he calls evidence and has made no opening speech he may then address the court. Either party may make a second address with leave, but when leave is given to one it may not be refused to the other. If both parties address the court twice, the prosecutor must do so the second time before the defence.

On the hearing of a complaint the same rules apply save that where the defendant obtains leave for a second address he must make it before the complainant makes his second speech (Magistrates' Courts Rules 1968, rr. 13, 14).

Submission of no case to answer

In a civil court a defendant who indicates his intention to submit that he has no case to answer will be put upon his election as to whether or not he wishes to rely upon such a submission or to call evidence; he cannot do both. In a criminal court, however, he is not subject to any such election, and if he makes an unsuccessful submission of no case to answer, he may continue with the case as if such submission had not been made. If he makes a submission, however, the opponent has the right of rely on points of law, although not upon the facts. It is very often necessary to exercise control over advocates exercising such a right to reply on the law, as there is a grave predisposition on their part to use it as an opportunity to have another attack upon the facts. Take care, however, that you limit your submissions of "no case to answer" to those which fully justify such a course. I have seen some so-called advocates who regard their mere presence in court as requiring a submission. Not only, is this a fearful waste of time and money, but the advocates reputation becomes such that when he so submits in a proper case his speech carries no weight.

On the other hand there are still too many magistrates who pay insufficient attention to such submissions, particulars where the case will otherwise be committed for trial. It is worth remembering that nothing is more calculated to persuade such a court to pay due regard to the legal requirements than to refer them to statements of the higher courts or the judges, in particular the Lord Chancellor, the Lord Chief Justice and the Master of the Rolls.

For example, you might refer then to a Practice Note of February 9, 1962, in the Law Reports where Lord Parker C.J., said:

"A submission that there is no case to answer may properly be made and upheld:

(a) when there has been no evidence to prove an essential element in the alleged offence or

(b) when the evidence adduced by the prosecution has been so discredited as a result of cross-examination or is so manifestly unreliable that no reasonable tribunal could safely convict on it.

Apart from these two situations a tribunal should not in general be called on to reach a decision as to the conviction or acquittal until the whole of the evidence—which either side wishes to tender has been placed before it. If, however, a submission is made that there is no case to answer, the decision should depend not so much on whether the adjudicating tribunal (if compelled to do so) would at that stage convict or acquit but on whether the evidence is such that a reasonable tribunal might convict."

Relying on submission

Difficult decisions have sometimes—although not frequently—to be taken as to whether or not to call the defendant or other witnesses to give evidence. This problem arises if you have made a submission of no case which has not been upheld; or where, although a case has been made against your client, you believe you can explain the circumstances in a way different from that relied upon by the plaintiff or the prosecutor. It may also arise, in its most acute form, where, although a prima facie case has been made out against your client, there are dangers in calling him as a witness because he may be destroyed in cross-examination. This is truly the moment of truth in the practice of advocacy, when you will require more courage, confidence and initiative than almost at any other time when the occasion arises to make decisions. General guidance cannot be given, since each situation must depend upon its own particular facts. If, exercising the best judgment you can, you are confident that your submission of no case should have succeeded, then you politely tell the court that you do not propose to call any evidence; that you will rely upon the submission you have made—whereupon you have the right, if you so wish, to address the court again as at the conclusion of the whole of the evidence. If you still fail to convince the court, then nothing is left but to go to the Court of Appeal, the Divisional Court or the Crown Court (as the case may be) to put the matter right. Unless you feel super-abundantly confident with the correctness of your submission, it is better to call your evidence and take the risk that your client may fill in some of the gaps and, in the process, lose his case. There is always the chance that he may increase such doubts as might have arisen, and resolve the matter in his own favour.

It does sometimes occur, as I have already indicated, that facts emerge in the course of your opponent's case in a way which enables you to tell the court that you do not dispute them. If so, you should count yourself fortunate indeed, since the most telling advocacy or a submission of "no case to answer" can result from inducing a court to adopt a slightly different slant, emphasis or construction in relation to the evidence so as to show that what was believed to be adverse to your client is, in fact, wholly favourable.

Calling the defendant client

The problem of whether or not to call your client when a prima facie case has been made out, but you are fearful that he may destroy his own chances of success, is a wholly different problem and, perhaps, creates the most intense difficulties of all. For the most part, the defendant who does not go into the witness box puts himself at a grave disadvantage. Human nature being what it is, the court—whether it consists of a lawyer or of laymen—will tend, however much it may fight against it, to assume that the defendant has something to hide. This you must squarely face, since all the probabilities are that if he does not go into the witness box it is because he indeed has something to hide. The only general guidance which can, with safety, be given is that one should hesitate long before failing to put the client into the witness box but many accused have been acquitted who did not do so.

Clarity of expression

In addressing a court, or at any stage of the proceedings, and particularly when you come to the closing speeches, it is essential that you should have acquired the ability to think on your feet. This is not to be confused with thinking with your feet, which occasionally appears to be the wont of some advocates. This is not a technique which one naturally possesses. I personally recommend, as I did, that one joins some reliable debating society in order to acquire this facility. I will recall that when I first began attempting to speak to a motion in such a society my problem was not, as experienced by some, a difficulty in starting, but a very considerable difficulty in finishing. I can well recall a sense of panic as I found myself, almost against my will, rambling on in an incomprehensible fashion—not even convincing myself—whilst desperately endeavouring to find some point upon which I could justifiably sit down. I have no doubt that my less kind critics would say that I have not materially changed over the years. Once again, however, I discovered that the answer lies in preparation in advance. It is vitally essential that one has either in writing, or certainly in one's mind, a skeletal plan of where one is to begin the arguments which one is proposing to develop—the points to be canvassed in the course of the arguments, and the point upon which one is intending to end.

I have already stressed the necessity of ensuring that any speech to a court has as its cardinal features simplicity and clarity of expression. If you, as an advocate, appear bored with your subject, and insincere about the integrity of your case and arguments, it is not to be expected that a court will feel any differently about them.

Final speeches

It is in relation to the final speeches that the analyses and the statement of objectives which I invited to you to compile at the very outset of your task can be of such enormous assistance to you. A properly prepared analysis and statement of objectives immediately provide an adequate framework around which to build your final address. You must, of course, take into account such changes as may be necessary, having regard to the different form in which the evidence may have revealed itself, or the variations in tactics which have become essential as the trial developed. Just as it is of great assistance to the court at the outset to draw the attention of the judge to the questions which he will be called upon to answer, it is a convenient way of concluding the trial to go back to those questions and, taking them one by one, to suggest to him, upon the basis of the evidence adduced, the proper conclusion which you feel able to invite him to reach in answer to the various questions which you postulated.

I recommend that during the course of the trial you should keep at all times at your side the analysis of facts and the statement of objectives, noting in a different coloured pencil the changes which have occurred as the trial has proceeded.

There will, doubtless, be many cases in which the evidence against your client will be so overwhelming that it will be virtually impossible to direct any sensible arguments in his favour. In those cases it is better to face reality. On the other hand, there are far too many advocates—including a large number of very great experience—who tend to collapse as soon as a case begins to move against them. Guard very much against this. There is nothing more distressing to a client, and nothing more dissatisfying to one who loses a cause, than to be left with the feeling that the best was not made of such case as he had.

If you can in the course of your address induce the tribunal to discuss the case with you, you will find that this will materially assist you in persuading the court towards your point of view. It will, at all events, enable you to ensure that whatever problems or doubts exist in the minds of the court, you have done your best to clarify them. You will find that lay justices will rarely, if ever, respond to such an invitation. High Court judges will often indicate the doubts which they would wish you to try to resolve. The Court of Appeal and the House of Lords tend to put direct questions to advocates, which as one would expect, usually go to the very nub of the case. Stipendiaries, county court judges and magistrates' clerks also will often interpose questions which they feel might usefully clarify the issue. By the same token, High Court and county court judges and stipendiary magistrates in particular will tend to indicate when they have grasped the point in order that you may not further develop it. This inclination on the part of a tribunal to discuss the legal problems involved and to curb unnecessary elaboration of arguments is of very great assistance to the administration of justice and to the technique of persuasion, and is the acid test of whether or not you are the master of the case you are presenting and have sufficiently dedicated yourself to becoming so. It also reflects one of the unquestionable advantages which a legally qualified judge has over the untrained justice of the peace who, lacking legal learning, is clearly unable to assist in this fashion.

Plea in mitigation

Yet, and we must face it, if the courts fail to gain assistance from advocacy in certain of its forms, *e.g.* in pleas in mitigation, the fault lies with the advocate and not the court. There are few activities in which the technique of persuasion can be more effectively brought to bear than in a mitigation plea—if properly handled. Moreover, if the courts found more of them helpful, they would be more anxious to grant legal aid to secure them. Once again, the pre-plea work is infinitely more important than the form of the plea itself. There are a number of advocates who, by a judicious use of language and histrionics, can often move to pity—so it seems—everyone in the court except the judge, who has generally already decided on the sentence before the plea in mitigation commences. Thus, in many cases, such a plea needs to be less directed to bringing the court to the right and just punishment, as jolting it from a predetermination to inflict what you may regard as the wrong one. While the situation is slowly improving, the sentencing procedure in this country, when compared to the infinite trouble taken to determine guilt, is still painfully inadequate. The court is given the barest of antecedents of the accused, which have generally been elicited from him by the police immediately after arrest, and when he is prone to be the least co-operative. Sometimes—and even now, when summary trial is included, the exceptions by far outnumber the cases where one is available—a probation report is procured. To this is added the record of previous convictions, if any. Always carefully read the probation report, although under existing conditions you will not generally see it until it is too late to correct wrong information included in it.

You may commence in the belief that you need to persuade the court to deal with the matter as you consider they should. In many cases, however, particularly the magistrates' court, your function is bound to involve persuading the magistrates to deal with it in some way different from that upon which they have already determined. This is not without its importance and arises because it is often the habit of magistrates when they retire to consider their decision on conviction to discuss penalty at the same time.

The Objective

As with other forms of advocacy, it is of prime importance to say to yourself, "What is the objective?" That does not mean "How can I get this man out who ought to be there for ten years?" but "What is the limited or general objective in regard to the mitigation which I am trying to put forward?" That involves, above all, trying consistently with fair and proper means to reduce the level of punishment which may come to your client but, secondly, and this is important, assisting the court to arrive at what seems to be the least punishment consistent with justice. No one will doubt that in seeking to persuade to the mitigation of punishment, the major requirement is to convince the court that you are there to assist, as indeed you are. The more and the sooner you can convince them that you are a rock the better. Not a rock like a millstone, as it were, about their neck, but a rock upon which they can firmly rest, someone to whom they can look for guidance on all matters about which they ought to know, and who can give them assistance on the disposal of the particular case. Start therefore, with this objective clearly in the forefront of your mind.

Next in importance is, of course, the preparation. I do not have any hesitation in repeating that in all forms of advocacy, and not least in mitigation, preparation is vital. True, it is an exercise, perhaps, more than any other form of advocacy, in which the way you present it is of great significance, but it is still the preparation before you rise to mitigate that will be decisive as to the effect you can have upon the court. It often needs more preparation, I suspect, than most advocates give to it, if a court is effectively to be brought to your way of thinking and the desires of your client, or at least half-way towards the desires of your client. This often means spending a great deal more time with the client than the average practitioner appears to believe solicitors need do. Frequently, and the time involved may not always be remunerated, I spend considerable time listening to a client, questioning him, trying to find out what, from the penological aspect, is vital. "Why," one must ask oneself, "does this person find himself in this trouble?" As a consequence I have discovered over the years that, even in those cases where I ultimately refer the client for some form of psychiatric investigation, I can now usually, more or less, ask the same sort of questions and frequently arrive at roughly the same sort of conclusions as psychiatrists do. Indeed, I have come to the view, although I hold psychiatrists (or some of them) in the greatest of respect, that many of the matters with which they are concerned can often be reduced to the application of simple psychology and common experience. In this regard, always try to get information about the client, not only from the client but from people who know him, and who may be able to give some insight into his problems, which even the probation officers, if and when they come to prepare their report, may lack.

The Mitigation

What then are the factors which you ought to consider in relation to mitigation? The first important matter is the age of the defendant. It is obviously relevant to such a plea whether the defendant is a person of whom it can be said, by reason of his age, that he has behaved in a way in which he might not have behaved given a few more years experience for life. But age in years can, in mitigation, also be deceptive; it is the experience of those who practise in this field that a considerable amount of crime can be traced to immaturity. Many people, despite their age in years, have not, in fact, grown up; they have not faced up to the responsibilities of life and, if this is so and you can demonstrate it, you can make a plea in mitigation in a highly effective way; it is something which judges and experienced magistrates know and to which they will be receptive. Properly presented and cogently argued, they may accept it as an explanation. Moreover, if it appears he has reached the stage where he is rapidly growing up, this provides an additional point in mitigation and it may be proper to urge that shutting him away from the stresses of life for a long period may well arrest, rather than assist, his further development.

Secondly, consider the defendant's domestic circumstances and his childhood. We have all, I expect, heard "pleas in mitigation" which, when analysed, come down to little more than this: "True, he may have raped this old lady; true he stole her money and she is still in hospital; he is, however, I must tell you, a very good boy to his mother." This is not mitigation; it is regurgitation. The vital key to successful mitigation, is still elimination and if you have nothing more to say than that, it would be better to say nothing at all. When, therefore, you come to consider these aspects of the matter, the defendant's background, his domestic circumstances and his childhood, put forward on the defendant's behalf only those points which are cogent and persuasive; which can be demonstrated as actually bearing upon the crime he has committed and support your plea that he should be dealt with in a certain way.

The Explanation

Thirdly, there is the defendant's attitude. Too often, advocates at the end of a case say (largely because they believe it is customary to do so) "I am instructed by the defendant to tell you he is very sorry for what he has done"; they fear to look over their shoulder in case the defendant is laughing his head off. If, every time you go into court, before the same bench of magistrates or judge, you assert the defendant's sorrow for what he has done, it is soon recognised that what you really mean is not so much that he is sorry for what he has done, but that he is sorry that he did it in such a ham-handed way that somebody caught him. When he receives his sentence, his sorrow is the greater—for having retained you to mitigate. Spend time, therefore, ascertaining whether he is truly sorry for what he has done, if he is not, forget it. The keynote to a plea is sincerity. If you can convince the court that you have discussed it with the defendant at length, and can enlarge on why he is sorry for his conduct, conveying to them, with sincerity, that what you are saying has the ring of truth, your statement that he has assured you it will never occur again carries some weight.

Another factor is the circumstances which led the defendant to commit the offence but, again this is to be used with discernment. To say, for example, that he was led to commit an offence of stealing £3,000 due to his fascination with sailing, which caused him desperately to want a new yacht, is not particularly convincing; on the other hand (and I take the simplest example), there may be mitigation that a child stole bread because he was excessively hungry. What is required is a critical and methodical examination of the true facts. I recall the case of a young girl four times convicted of shoplifting. On the fourth occasion she did it in what can only be described as an exceedingly incompetent and obvious way. Moreover, the last offence was committed while she was on probation. She was interviewed three times and, on one of the occasions, with her boyfriend with whom she was living. In the result, it appeared that she was living in a state of some mental turmoil. She was devoted to her parents whom she knew would be heartbroken that she was living, as Ethel M. Dell might have said, "in sin." Her boyfriend wanted to marry her, but she was uncertain whether she was ready to marry. There seemed little doubt that the reason why she dashed off and committed these offences of shoplifting, under conditions where her arrest was almost inevitable (offences which are sometimes committed from greed but very often for other reasons), was largely an outlet for her intense mental confusion and frustration. It was what psychologists call "a cry for help." In practice, and this I must stress, it is in ascertaining of facts of this type—of the circumstances under which the defendant came to commit the offence—that one has one's greatest opportunity for putting forward effective mitigation.

The Severity

Other relevant factors are the nature of the offence, and whether the type of offence is prevalent. Of course, if there have been an enormous number of burglaries in a locality, it is hardly persuasive to the local bench in a plea for leniency that your client says that, although he may have committed many other crimes of dishonesty, this is the first time he has committed burglary. It is even less mitigation to say that he was attracted to the offence by the fact that as there are so many burglaries in the area he thought he ought to get into the act. If, in fact, there are a lot of burglaries in the area, you have to be

144

conscious of the fact that the bench may be inclined to hit those who commit burglaries more than other offences and you will have to find some way of showing some exceptional reason why your client should not be dealt with in a severe manner. For example, it is clearly relevant that he acted under the domination or coercion of others; in the case of an affray that he was on the periphery of it and not the organiser, or that he was led into committing whichever offence is involved by other older and more experienced people.

That the time spent in custody may be a mitigating factor speaks for itself, and is clearly something which should be looked into and, if appropriate, mentioned. You should also have regard to whether a probation officer has seen the defendant. If he has not, and it is a suitable case, it is often wise to approach the probation officer and, if he will do it, ask him to see the defendant in advance. It is, however, important to know your court; there are some courts which are greatly influenced by what a probation officer says, and some which are not. If one of the former, it is a good thing to say that you have taken the opportunity of asking the probation officer to see the defendant; that the probation officer has done so and then to call the probation officer or invite the court to do so. It is often wise to get in first so that the probation officer may consider the matters which, in your careful preparation, you have decided are particularly relevant. You should also consider whether you need to cross-examine any of the prosecution witnesses in order to bring out mitigating circumstances. In rare cases, the defendant might be advised to plead not guilty in order that a full and clear picture should emerge. This, I stress, is only rarely desirable, because, by and large, experience shows that by fighting cases which should be the subject of a plea, you bring out many facts which are damaging to your client. Occasionally, however, where the defendant is not deeply involved and where some explanation will emerge which may assist in mitigation, it is wise to enter a plea of not guilty for the purpose of bringing those matters out.

The Attitude of the Judiciary

I turn to a sixth possible mitigating factor, one which I regard as perhaps the most important of all, and that is the arrangements which can be made to reduce or eliminate the risk of repetition of the offence. Magistrates and judges are not looking for grounds for sending a person to prison; quite the contrary is generally the case. The approach, although I am not saying this is absolutely uniform, is that if the court can find some reason for dealing with the case in a more lenient way, it will. Under current conditions, the one thing about which a court is particularly concerned is whether, consistent with its duty to the public and having regard to the chances of a repetition of the offence, it can take a more lenient view than it otherwise would. It is, therefore, important that you direct your mind to this aspect, particularly in a case likely to involve a custodial sentence. Is the defendant's environment wrong and, if it is, can arrangements be made to get him out of it? Can a responsible witness be called who will say the defendant will live with him and that he will take care to see that he does not commit the offence again? Has the defendant been in company which ought no longer to be available to him, and, if so, what steps can be taken to see that he will no longer be in that company? Is the defendant subject to stresses and strains which have led him into trouble, from which it can be shown it is possible to remove him? Does the defendant need medical help, and is it available? These facts are vital, more perhaps than any other factor, in persuading the court to take a less serious view in terms of punishment.

Having mentioned the possible need for medical treatment, I would stress that this must not be over done. If you are one of those who believe that all crime is really a manifestation of mental disease, then, at least, keep the thought to yourself, and do not convey it to the court. Certainly, in my view, it is not true. Crime is committed for a variety of reasons and high on the list, as I have said, are immaturity and greed. Only when there is a cogent case for saying that the particular defendant needs medical treatment or that a doctor could help, should you use it. Moreover, if it involves psychiatric questions, secure one of the few psychiatrists who have their feet on the ground. It is most difficult if you call a psychiatrist as a witness, if, every now and again, you have to lift up your hand and pull him down. Obtain someone who knows where the ground is, who has enough weight to remain firmly on it, and who will only put forward sensible, reliable opinions and not merely opinions biased towards the defendant. The psychiatrists who carry weight in the court are those who it is known, when reduced to it, will say frankly that having seen the defendant on several occasions, they really do not know what can be done for him, but who, at the end, say they believe that it might be reasonable to try this, or that, approach. When witnesses of this calibre are able to make positive recommendations they are more readily accepted by reason of their known reluctance to do so in less manageable cases. Do not hesitate, if you do get an unreliable medical report, to telephone the psychiatrist, and tell him his report will not impress the court, and could he modify it slightly. For example, to explain that you do not want him to alter his opinion, but would he make it plain to the court that he recognises that it is not his responsibility but that of the court to fix the punishment?

Over recent years one faces a new problem in mitigating. The media has become highly critical of many judicial decisions, much of which can be misconceived and misinformed. As a result, sentencers now tend—even subconsciously—to take into account, in some classes of offence, the likely media reaction. You should consider whether, in the appropriate case, you should boldly refer, in polite terms, to this aspect, stressing that the test is what the court considers to be the correct sentence, and not the media. Needless to say, this calls for a careful choice of words and tact.

Admissions

Finally, on this aspect of the matter, always contact the prosecution as to any facts which might be dangerous to your client. You have a special advantage here, when it comes to mitigation; if you are able to say that you are contemplating advising the defendant to plead guilty and that time may be saved, the faces of prosecutors tend to light up and they may be, as indeed they often are in other circumstances, helpful in indicating to you factors which may affect the decision of the court and which may not be known to you. Always, therefore, if you are defending, have a word with the prosecution. I would also remark, speaking now to prosecutors, that if a defendant is going to plead guilty and there is something which might assist him (not to cheat justice, but to secure it in terms of sentence), it is proper to tell the defence advocate of the relevant facts. Certainly, the defence should ascertain from the prosecution whether there is anything likely to take them by surprise. Something which often does take you by surprise, if you are not exceedingly careful, is whether or not your client has previous convictions. If a man says he has only got two previous convictions, it may be a hundred to one that he has got five. If he says he has no previous convictions, it is possible that he is right; however, never believe him, always check with the prosecution.

I turn now to the question of presentation, and first I would say: know the court. If you do not practise in that particular court, find out as best you can by enquiry as to the court's attitude on particular aspects. It is of vital importance to know, before you address a court, whether it particularly dislikes the sort of offence involved; if so, you have to distinguish your case from those with which the court normally deals in a severe way. Certainly, if it is a lay bench of magistrates, try to find out what is likely to be their approach to the particular problem.

Ensure that you know the statutory punishment. It indicates that you are in command of the situation if you are able to tell the bench what are the alternatives open to them and go through them, one by one, explaining why you suggest they should not resort to a particular punishment. If you deal with it in this fashion, it does at least show you have given your mind to the subject which they have to determine. It is amazing the number of occasions in which not only the defence does not know, but if the bench asks the prosecutor he does not know what is the penalty involved and the court has to wait until the clerk looks it up. That should not be. It is part of the preparation; indeed it is difficult to know how you can make up your own mind what to urge upon a bench if you have not yourself looked it up beforehand.

The Psychology

I have mentioned earlier the need for elimination, for conciseness and cogency but I want to mention it again. There are some cases which, frankly, are beyond mitigation, and in those cases it is almost impossible to say anything sensible. There is one further ploy which for some almost inexplicable psychological reason sometimes works. If you know the bench and you know the sort of things they are going to say, it is often wise where it is impossible to advance anything good, to say, "Well you know, your worships, this really is a dreadful case; I have given much thought as to how best I can present this matter on behalf of my client, but I realise, things being as they are in regard to this class of offence, your worships must of necessity take a very serious view of this matter" and so on. This, at least, will give you the opportunity to advance a plea for such compassion as the court can justifiably extend. But if you take out of the mouth of the magistrates the very things they were waiting to say and end with a plea for leniency, they, sometimes, for some curious psychological reason, may deal with it in a much more lenient way than they otherwise would have done. Certainly in a much more lenient way than if, when they are thinking that this is a man who has got to be dealt with severely, you come into direct collision with their minds so that they are repelled and encouraged to make things a little worse. It is only in a truly desperate case that I would advise this course, but it is worth remembering and the extent to which you use it is obviously your affair, regarding the simple psychology involved.

The application of psychology applies not only to trying to understand the bench, but trying to understand how the bench will react to you. As already observed, one key to persuasion is to make those whom you are trying to persuade believe that what you want them to do is something they thought of themselves. No one is ever more pleased to decide something in a particular way than if he believes that all the kudos is going to him for having thought of it. If, in your plea, you can lead the court through various possibilities so that it appears to be seizing on one of them of its own volition, you are much more likely to persuade it to that course than if you go at it like a bull at a gate. Do not, on the other hand, for a moment be put off in an appropriate case by the old and traditional wives tale that it is wrong to say to a court "In my submission you should deal with this matter in this way." Some appear to regard that as improper advocacy. I know of no warrant for it. If your arguments are sound, the conclusions which you draw from them are no sounder for being hesitantly expressed.

Another aspect of psychology is the quality of evident frankness, for instance, by referring, with the client's permission, to previous convictions when there is no obligation to disclose them.

If it is probable—or even possible—that the court may be guided or persuaded to deal with your case by way of a monetary penalty; against that possibility ensure that you have ascertained, in advance, the fullest particulars as to the defendant's means. This involves not only ascertaining his income and take-home pay, but also the necessary expenses which he has to incur. If, moreover, you have any documents which confirm the information which you have obtained, have them readily to hand, in case the figures which you provide are questioned. Always ensure that any documents which it is essential to have with you, are readily available. For example, in a motoring case, remind the client to bring his driving licence with him, and ask him for it before the case commences, bearing in mind that, in the majority of motoring cases, the court is unable to conclude the matter until the driving licence is produced.

The measure of a court's confidence in you and the degree of reliance it can place on you is directly related to the efficiency with which you conduct the case in hand.

The Duty

Finally a plea in mitigation on behalf of those—at whatever level—who sit in a judicial capacity. Do not take the view that having agreed to sit in judgment on their fellow men they deserve whatever comes to them. Rather recognise that they are performing an important public duty—the administering of justice—and some are doing it at their own expense in money and time.

Do, therefore, try to search for an original, attractive and interesting approach for your plea in mitigation. Do reduce what you have to say to a minimum; do ensure that your facts are accurate and your deductions from them trustworthy; do remember that your task is to help and not to hinder—to persuade and not to dictate; to be sincere and informed and, above all, to play your own important part in bringing justice to the particular case balanced against the interests of your client on the one hand and the public on the other.

Guilty plea

The public are little enough aware of the heart-searching and anxiety which the legal profession face before deciding to advise a client, in a civil cause, to throw in his hand, or, in a criminal case, to plead guilty. In legally aided civil litigation the situation is, to some extent, ameliorated for the legal adviser because, under the Legal Aid legislation, he is under a duty in order to protect the interests of the legal aid fund to draw to the attention of the Legal Aid Committee the hopelessness of a case as soon as it becomes apparent. To that extent the decision is partly taken out of his hands and put into those of that Committee. In criminal cases the situation is somewhat different. Although, since the Criminal Justice Act of 1967, there is a Complaints Tribunal, and it may be that a lawyer who persistently fought hopeless cases without justification, might conceivably be brought before that tribunal, the control which might be exercised by those responsible for administering criminal legal aid is much more tenuous.

It therefore behoves every advocate to ensure threat he does not persist, on the insistence of the client, in contesting criminal causes merely because the expense is falling upon the State and not upon the individual. There has been a dramatic and understandable change in the attitude of defendants since the advent of legal aid. Dr. Johnson said that nothing more concentrated a man's mind than the knowledge that he was going to be hanged and, to this might be added that nothing more induces a man to terminate litigation than the knowledge that the expense will come out of his own pocket. With that sanction gone there is an increasing tendency on the part of defendants in criminal cases to fight on, in the vain hope that something may turn to their advantage, but in the knowledge that if all fails the expense will not fall upon them.

Moreover, some advocates appear little enough to realise that a needlessly contested case may do harm to the client. Contrary to an earlier decision of the Court of Criminal Appeal, it is now recognised that the fact that an accused has not wasted the time of the court; has not

151

gone into the witness box to commit perjury; and has not thrown the expense of a trial upon the State, are significant factors to be taken into account in reducing the length of the sentence. Indeed, a competent advocate needs strongly to impress upon the court, in a case where he has, within the limits permitted to him, prevailed upon his client to enter a plea of guilty, that this is a factor which the court should take into account in the client's favour. But a court may not increase a penalty because an accused pleaded not guilty.

There may, of course, be cases where an inexperienced advocate may have difficulty in deciding whether it is appropriate to take the course here indicated. In those circumstances he is well advised to discuss his problem with a more experienced colleague. Indeed, this may be said of all problems in relation to advocacy, where such a course is possible, since nothing does more to clear one's own mind that the submission of a series of facts or propositions of law or the details of a particular problem to a fresh and independent mind. One need only add, in this connection, underlining what I have said before, that in the conduct of your advocacy in the future much will depend, so far as the particular court is concerned, upon the reputation which you have established by your advocacy in the past. Never under-estimate the intelligence of your opponent and, above all, never under-estimate the intelligence of the court. If you are seen repeatedly to be fighting, on legal aid, cases which a prudent advocate would have dealt with on a plea of guilty, you will inevitably undermine the confidence of the court in your integrity, and all the disadvantages which I have previously outlined, as flowing from that unhappy situation, will be heaped upon your head.

You may, however, find that not the least of your difficulties is to convince your client that it is in his best interests to plead guilty. This also involves a technique, since while you must satisfy him that the consequences of his guilt have become inescapable, you must never display such enthusiasm for the prosecution case that you undermine his confidence in you. The course which I follow, and which I recommend, involves four main principles. The first is to ensure that you have mastered, by patient study the intricacies of the case both against and (if any) for him. The second is to explain to him at the outset of the vital interview, and repeat from time to time, that you are going to play the role of Devil's Advocate in order to assess the case against him. The third principle is, as you take him through the points against him, to put his answer against them, and demonstrate—by implication, and only rarely, directly, that his contentions will not prevail. If you merely tell him that his case is hopeless and he must plead guilty, you will probably do no more than drive him to more pliant advisers. Having demonstrated the weakness of the case, you should illustrate, by comparison, the powerful mitigation which can be provided from the material which he regards as affording an answer. Show the advantages of putting forward his explanation without any risk of it being contradicted, against the dangers of putting it in evidence and having it rejected. Point out that it would be better for him to contest the case, if he is satisfied there is any real chance of success, but that it will be the worse for him if the judge or magistrates form an adverse view of him because they believe (where appropriate, adding for tact, even wrongly) that he may be lying. Finally, if he agrees to plead and is unreliable, get him to sign a statement that he has made that decision after all the aspects have been fully discussed and explained to him.

Application for bail

Certainly many newly qualified lawyers will be required to make applications for bail. No less than other forms of advocacy, this calls for careful preparation and thought. Observation seems to indicate that insufficient of either or both is too often the case.

Nothing is ever lost by communicating with the prosecuting solicitors (where they are instructed) or the Police Officer in charge of the case in order to ascertain in advance whether there will be any objection to bail and, if so, on what grounds. The worst that may happen is that the information will not be divulged and, in the vast majority of cases, considerable assistance will be given in this connection—as indeed it should be.

When the grounds of objection are positively known or accurately assessed, it may be possible to obtain either evidence or create conditions which will lessen or obviate the force of the objections. For example, if it is said that the defendant has no permanent address, it may be possible to produce evidence to the contrary or, alternatively, to give assurances that he has arranged for residence with some reliable person during the pendency of the case.

The practice on the hearings of applications for bail vary in different parts of the country. In the metropolitan area, both in stipendiary and lay magistrates' courts, the police will be asked whether there is any objection to bail and, if there is, the officer will at once go to the witness box and state the grounds for objection. The advocate for the defendant may then cross-examine him before addressing the bench. In some places outside London, as soon as it is discovered there is police objection to bail, the advocate for the defendant is called upon to make his application. Unless he is wary, he will find that the grounds for objection will not be advanced until he has concluded his application and the advocate will have neither opportunity to cross-examine the officer nor the right to reply and deal with the actual objections which have been advanced. If that is the procedure of the court it is one that requires early reform, but, meanwhile, it is quite imperative that immediately upon rising to make the application, the advocate should ask whether there is an objection to bail and, if so, whether he might first hear from the prosecution as to the grounds for objection, and ask to question the police officer, thereby placing himself in exactly the same position as would be the case if the matter were heard in the metropolitan area.

Objections to bail tend to fall broadly into three categories: there are those where, because of the seriousness of the charge, or the possibility that the defendant might abscond, or both the prosecution bona fide believe that it is necessary to remand in custody. The second group are those cases where the prosecution do not seriously object to bail but, against the remote possibility that the defendant will not ultimately appear, are unwilling to take the responsibility of consenting to bail and prefer to place the responsibility on to the court; these cases are far more numerous than might otherwise be believed. The third and last category are those, less frequent but not uncommon, in which the police either prefer to have the defendant in custody to facilitate further interrogation or are using the objection to bail as an instrument to induce the defendant to greater cooperation in the hope that, if this is forthcoming in the way the police would wish, the objection will be lifted. It is important to make a critical assessment as to the precise category into which the objections fall; certainly it is a mistake to approach the cross-examination of the police officers concerned upon the basis that the third alternative is always applicable (and too many advocates appear universely to assume this to be so) when the objections more likely fall into the first alternative.

Stipendiary magistrates are much more inclined to overrule police objections to bail than lay magistrates. Some country Benches appear to rely heavily upon the views of the police as to bail. In those courts it is not improper to remind the Bench, in a tactful way, that the responsibility is entirely theirs.

The considerations which arise when a court is deciding whether to grant bail are:
- (i) The nature of the accusation;
- (ii) The nature of the evidence in support of the accusation;
- (iii) The severity of the punishment which conviction will entail;
- (iv) The financial and social integrity of the sureties.

Although it has been said that it is not usual to grant bail on charges of murder (*Re Barthelemy*, 1 E. & B. 8), this is on the basis of an old case and bail is sometimes granted under modern conditions, bearing in mind that the charge is no longer subject to the death penalty. It will often be granted in the case of "mercy killings" but an important consideration in those cases and others where there is a mental element involved is to consider not only the safety of the public, but, no less, the safety of the defendant.

It was said by the Court of Criminal Appeal (*R.* v. *Dyson* (1943) 29 Cr.App.R. 104) that it is desirable, when evidence of a defendant's previous convictions is being placed before a court considering the question of bail, that such evidence should be submitted in writing rather than give viva voce in open court. This rule is rarely observed and advocates would be well advised in appropriate cases, to draw the court's attention to it.

You should familiarise yourself with section 128 of the Magistrates Courts Act 1980, which deals with the court's powers to remand in custody or on bail, section 20 of the Criminal Justice Acts of 1967 and 1982 which imposes restrictions on the refusal of bail. It is quite proper, and often wise, respectfully to remind the court that the provisions of the Criminal Justice Acts were designed to ensure that fewer persons were needlessly remanded in custody and that it occasions undue hardship if a person—who is still presumed innocent—is placed in prison, although he may later be acquitted, or even, if convicted, not sent to custodial detention.

You should also be familiar with the sections of the Police and Criminal Evidence Act, 1984, which give the police special powers to detain and further detain, also the provisions as to custody in sections 46 and 47 of the Act.

After you have made several applications for bail on behalf of different clients you will find that the arguments which you must advance may appear to have become repetitive and stereotyped. This is not your fault; it is because the objections to bail which are generally advanced are themselves repetitive and stereotyped. For example, it may be said "the defendant will interfere with witnesses." In cross-examination you may ascertain that there is no evidence to support this allegation other than a sudden rush of intuition to the mind of the officer; that he has already obtained signed statements from the witnesses and, if he has not done so, it is solely his fault that this is so. The apparently cogent argument that the accused has a number of previous convictions may be offset by eliciting in cross-examination or advancing in argument that on these occasions he was granted bail and did not abscond or otherwise misbehave. Against the assertion that "the police have not yet completed their enquiries" it may be observed that this does not constitute a ground for increasing bail. It may be a valid ground for increasing the numbers of an excessively overworked police force, but not for incarcerating a citizen until that happy state is achieved.

In appropriate cases you may invite the court, as a condition of granting bail, to require substantial sureties (whom you have available and whose names and addresses you have previously given to the police to enable them to check their reliability); to require the defendant to report regularly to the police; to surrender the defendant's passport (a futile, but often, acceptable condition, since yearly passports can be obtained virtually on demand from post offices); that there shall be a condition of residence in a particular place or any other condition likely to render probable his appearance on his trial.

As always, however, there is another side to the coin. It is unwise to pursue an application for bail where commonsense dictates that no responsible court could be expected to grant it. By displaying your reasonableness and sense of responsibility at the first remand (where you are convinced you would not succeed) and telling the magistrates why you do not apply, you will greatly strengthen your hand when later you do apply. Moreover, if there is likely to be a series of remands, given careful thought to an appeal to a Judge in Chambers. If you take this step in other than a strong case, you will render it unlikely that you can subsequently persuade the magistrates to change their minds once they have been fortified by the refusal of a High Court Judge.

Since the Bail Act 1976 a court is required to grant bail unless the exceptions set out in the first Schedule to the Act are present. Moreover, the Divisional Court has said that a renewed application should not be made for bail, if a court has already directed that a relevant exception has justified the refusal of bail, unless there are new facts or considerations which were not previously before the court. It is suggested that the latter words do not preclude an application being made on pre-existing facts, where some consideration which was thus available was not advanced due to oversight or some other reason. However, it has always been very much to your client's advantage if you adduce some significant fact or facts which were not known when the earlier application was made and which, therefore, distinguishes and enhances the quality of the application.

If you are representing the prosecution, take every point of objection which has its basis in fact and responsibility and advance no objection in which you yourself lack confidence when judged objectively.

Above all, when applying for bail, both in cross-examination and argument, remember that your best chance of success lies in displaying such moderation and responsibility that the objections are made to look the more unreasonable and unjust.

Conclusion

Such then, I suggest, is the stuff of which the technique of persuasion is made. The work of the advocate is an honourable pursuit, of very great value, which will bring a great and intense degree of satisfaction, whilst on other occasions it will fill the well-meaning and earnest advocate with feelings of despair. One would hesitate long before disagreeing with anyone of the eminence of Lord MacMillan. He, however, has pointed out that an advocate, in pleading a case, does not express his own opinions. That, of course, is clear beyond doubt. He goes on to say, in *Law and Other Things*, that "it is his business to present to the court all that his client would have said for himself if he had possessed the requisite skill and knowledge." I would seek to quarrel with the words "all" and "would" in that context. Whatever the skill and knowledge of a man who is pleading his own cause, he is prone to introduce a great deal of matter which is best left out. I would prefer to say, in so far as elimination is such a vital part of effectively employing the technique of persuasion, that it is the business of the advocate to present to the court what his client *should* say for himself if he possessed the requisite skill and knowledge.